WOMEN OF WEXFORD
1798–1998

By the same author:

The Windswept Shore: A History of the Courtown district (1982) (1995)
County Wexford in the Famine Years 1845–1849 (1995)

Published by: Courtown Publications, South Pier, Courtown Harbour, Co. Wexford
Cover design & typesetting: Andy Gilsenan, Dublin
Printed by: ColourBooks Dublin

Cover illustration

By kind permission of St. Senan's Parents group

A detail from the Women of Wexford Memorial Tapestry designed and woven in Enniscorthy by St. Senan's Parents Group as part of their 1798 Bi-centennial Commemorations. The tapestry symbolises nine generations of women standing on the old bridge across the river Slaney in the shadow of Vinegar Hill. The linked arms represent the spanning of two hundred years from 1798 to 1998.

My thanks to Group Co-ordinator Maeve McCauley,

Artist/Facilitator: Joanne Breen,

Group members: Margaret Bracken, Siobhan McGee, Eileen Galligan, Edel Hogan, Ann Dobbs, Kathleen Dobbs, Kathleen Doran, Edel Cahill, Edel Kinsella, Louise Doyle, Myra Weafer, Bridie Goff, Sheila Farrell, Bea Moorhouse and Julie Moorhouse O'Leary,

For my grandchildren, with love.

The Marriage of the Princess Aoife of Leinster with Strongbow by Daniel MacLise. By permission National Gallery of Ireland

Frontispiece

The marriage of Aoife MacMurrough to Richard FitzGilbert de Clare (Strongbow), Earl of Strigoil at Waterford on 25 August 1170, by Daniel Maclise is reproduced here by courtesy of the National Gallery of Ireland.

Arguably the most famous Wexford woman of all, the story of Aoife Mac Murrough remains unrecorded. Somewhere between the realms of myth and history we learn that Aoife was born at Ferns, daughter of Diarmuid MacMurrough, King of Leinster and Sive O'Faolain. Sive was the second wife of Diarmuid according to the rights of the Brehon Law. His first wife was Mor O'Toole, sister of Laurence, Abbot of Glendalough and later Archbishop of Dublin. Diarmuid's family consisted of Mor, his first wife; Uraclam and Enna, her daughter and son respectively; his second wife Sive, another son Conor and two more daughters Aoife and Dervorgilla and Donal MacMurrough Kavanagh, his natural son, born outside marriage.

In 1167 MacMurrough, having enlisted aid from Richard Fitzgilbert de Clare, (Strongbow) Earl of Strigoil, returned to Ferns to await the arrival of the Normans. Part of Diarmuid's bargain was a promise of succession to Leinster for Strongbow who was to marry Aoife. Strongbow was a middle-aged widower with two children Gilbert and Isabella by his first wife Isabella.

Strongbow landed near Waterford in 1170 and his marriage to Aoife, solemnised by the Bishop of Waterford, took place in the Cathedral there. The following year Diarmuid MacMurrough died suddenly at Ferns and on the arrival in Wexford of King Henry II of England, Strongbow was confirmed in the lands of Leinster to hold them in the King's name. These comprised the five modern counties of Wexford, Carlow, Laois, Kilkenny and Kildare.

Aoife's life with Strongbow was short and turbulent. She had sons of the marriage before 1176 when Richard Fitzgilbert de Clare died and was buried in Christ Church Dublin; a cathedral he had built.

Aoife was still a young woman when Strongbow died and she continued to live in a fortress tower at Cappamore County Waterford. The year of her death is not known.

Contents

Acknowledgments

I am indebted, for information on the women included in this study to the following, who generously contributed their time and knowledge and gave me permission to publish: Lady Anita Ainsworth, Nicholas and Kathleen Breen, Sisters M. Eugenie Brennan and Anne Harpur of Sisters of the Institute of St. John of God and Sister Mary Blake, Central Archivist, IBVM (Loreto), Bernard Browne, David Carbury, Director County Museum, Enniscorthy, Ann Corrigan, ICA, Nicholas Cosgrave, Michael Dempsey, Wexford County Library, Irene Elgee, Betty Glavey and the Ryan family, John Graby Director, RIAI, Alice Griffen, Department of Agriculture, the Kissane family, Peig Kinsella, Frances Murphy, Hilary Murphy, Josie McGarry, James Quirke, Aidan Ryan, Nicholas Furlong, George Bridges, Sean Furlong, Aidan Wafer and James Whitworth. All were unstinting in supplying material and photographs without which this book could not have been written.

A special word of thanks is due to Fionnuala Hanrahan, County Librarian and to Celestine Rafferty of Wexford County Library, for their willing help. Thanks also to Mark Carry and to my son Tim for giving me the benefit of their computer expertise and last but not least to Lewis, my husband, for his unfailing support and encouragement.

Introduction

This book focuses on Wexford women who lived in the two centuries from 1798 to 1998. They played diverse and worthwhile roles in an Irish society which was patriarchal as was similar in most European countries of the day. To be born female had tremendous consequences in social, political and economic terms. Women had no independent legal capacity in a world where men alone controlled the political and commercial life of the country.

The role of woman, in the main, was performed within a domestic context and depended largely on class. Women were viewed as weak in mind and body and depended for status on fathers and husbands. Apart from the religious life there was just one perceived role for women; that of wives and mothers who had taken a marriage vow to "love, honour and obey" their husbands. Those husbands were in many cases significantly older than their wives and required the approval of her father. Very often she had little choice in the matter.

Women in the landed gentry class were more likely to be remembered as they were to be found on committees for the relief and improvement of the poor and were therefore recorded, while others, less well-off financially, were absorbed in day to day existence and provision for their families.

The Catholic Relief Act 1793 extended the franchise to "adult males" only. A Reform Act in 1867 specifically mentioned "man" in connection with the vote. It was not until 1879 that women were first admitted to study for university degrees and a number of Wexford women were among the earliest to take advantage of the opportunity.

In the twentieth century, women in business and the professions replaced themselves in the home with trusted domestics who in a great number of instances came to be regarded as family members. Domestic servants were poorly paid.

The wives of business men often shared the management of the family business. A widow achieved a position of independence, when her husband died and left her with a life-interest in his property. She usually continued to run the business while rearing their children. Women who remained single had to earn a living and domestic service provided the best opportunity for this. A small number of women became governesses to the children of the wealthier middle and upper classes.

The most menial of jobs were carried out by women but that of "wet nurse" was lowest on the scale even beneath washing the dead or cleaning the workhouse toilets. Families were large and in rural districts farmers' wives, along with domestic chores and rearing children, were expected to milk cows, feed pigs, tend poultry and perform other laborious tasks around the farm. In 1797 Mary Ann McCracken wrote:

> I wish to know if they (women) have any rational ideas of liberty and equality for themselves or whether they are contented with their present abject and dependent situation, degraded by custom and education beneath their rank in society in which they were originally placed; for if we suppose woman was created for a companion for man, she must of course be his equal in understanding, as without equality of mind there can be no friendship and without friendship there can be no happiness in society.[1]

Centuries before her time, Mary Ann McCracken would have been at home in the vanguard of the modern women's movement for equality of the 1970s. Religious orders provided opportunities for able women to realise their talents and from the mid-nineteenth century women were involved in nursing the sick and the education of children.

In 1898, women got the right to vote in Local Government elections and the following year eighty-five women were elected to sit on the Boards of Poor Law Guardians; thirty-one of those women became Local District Councillors.[2] The Irishwomen Workers' Union was founded in 1911 and on 21 November 1918, women obtained a vote in Parliamentary elections.

Irrespective of class or religious denomination, the women in this study had some things in common. They were devout in the practice of their religion and loyal to churches which were repressive to women. All were pioneers in one way or another. Many were described, by those who knew them, as being "tight", "shrewd" and "tough". Perhaps words such as "thrifty", "intuitive" and "tenacious" would more appropriately describe their characteristics. More likely it is possible that, in their efforts to survive, they were resourceful, independent and self-sufficient. However, they were not conforming to the traditional perception of a woman's place which was, according to Archbishop McCabe of Dublin, "the seclusion of the home".[3]

There was no State support for those in need. These women rose to the demands placed on them by fortune and with fore-sight, expertise and a degree of risk-taking, handled the practical affairs of their lives. They were not found wanting in their ability to set up schools, hospitals, businesses and organisations yet despite an apparent "hard-headed" approach were described by those who knew them as being of charitable and caring disposition.

But the women in this book were the exception rather than the rule and albeit that there are many more women who deserve to be recorded, the reason these women are, is precisely because they were different and pushed out the parameters delineating the lives of women. They fought for the issues which were relevant to their lives and times and their achievements must be viewed in that context.

It must be remembered that in the past young women were conditioned to view work as an interim place between school and marriage and the marriage bar on civil servants and teachers re-inforced this attitude. Indeed many of the skills of women were undervalued. [4]

It was not until the 1970s that a real change began in society's view of a woman's place within the family and within society. The church's influence no longer dominated and its view that a woman's place is as wife, mother and home-maker is no longer relevant. The State's laws with regard to the behaviour of women are also being challenged.

The modern Irish woman is highly educated and well-informed combining home, family and career. Despite this many hold negative views about the effects on children of mothers working outside the home on a full-time basis. It could be argued that the creation of part-time work for both men and women might be worthwhile allowing both parents more time for their children.

Within society, however, there are still limitations on women and in the 1997 General Election only 20 women were returned as Dail Deputies out of 166 seats.[5] There were 23 women in the outgoing Dail. Wexford's only woman TD and Junior Minister Avril Doyle, lost her seat while five male candidates for the county were elected.

Women at work are often judged by male standards rather than on personal skills and behaviour. Perhaps it is time to define both men and women as individuals and stop putting them into gender brackets which require them to behave in a certain way.

Although the behaviour of men and women has changed in modern Ireland and is, in the main, no longer confined within traditionally defined roles, this change for example, is not apparent in the running of some sports Clubs where women are not yet accepted as equal members.

This is an effort to give an historical dimension to the part played by women, and in particular the women of Wexford, in Irish society. There were women involved in all aspects of life in Ireland from the 1798 Insurrection to the Famine, the language and literary revival, suffrage, the 1916 Rising and the feminist battles of the twentieth century; yet they are disregarded in the history books. These women pushed out the boundaries and became prominent in public and professional life, education, charities, farming, organisations, business, the arts, sports, etcetera.

No doubt there are other Wexford women worthy of inclusion here, however records of such women are difficult to find. Nevertheless many of us reared in the homes of County Wexford have always been aware that "the hand that rocked the cradle ruled the world".

Changes are happening slowly but not without effort. Mary Robinson noted in 1990, on her election as first woman President of Ireland, that in the last decade of the twentieth century, the women of Ireland "mna na h-Eireann. . . instead of rocking the cradle rocked the system" and the recent election of Mary McAleese as Ireland's second woman President re-inforces this statement.[6]

Finally it is hoped that this account of some "women of Wexford" will be not only of interest to the general reader but will play a part in putting more women onto the pages of history.

References:
(1) Mary McNeill *The Life and Times of Mary Ann McCracken* (1770-1866) pub 1988
(2) Margaret MacCurtain "Women, the vote and revolution" in Margaret MacCurtain and Donncha O Corrain eds *Women in Irish Society (The Historical Dimension)* (1978)
(3) (letter read at all Masses in the Archdiocese of Dublin in March 1881)
(4) Eunice McCarthy "Women and work in Ireland" in Margaret MacCurtain and Donncha O'Corrain eds. *Women in Irish Society (The Historical Dimension)* (1978)
(5) *Irish Times* 20/6/97
(6) Mary McAleese was inaugurated as Uachtaran na hEireann on 12/11/1997

Mary Breen (centre) with her daughters Maisie and Kit (1951)

Mary Breen (1890-1965)

Business woman and farmer

It was said of her that "if she threw a threepenny bit up in the air, a half-crown would come down". In the year in which the "uncrowned King of Ireland" Charles Stuart Parnell fell from grace and the O'Shea divorce suit held popular attention, Mary Redmond was born at Knocknascough, Ferns in 1890. She was one of a family of six, of Patrick Redmond, a farmer and Catherine Roche. With four brothers and one sister, she received her early education at the local National School.

In 1911, at the age of twenty-one Mary married John Breen; one of a family of twenty-one children and moved to live in Ballydonegan Ferns. There were six sons of their marriage; Peter, Pat, John, Tom, Martin, Nick and three daughters, Frances, Maisie and Kitty. Her husband, many years her senior, had years of bad health and died of tuberculosis on 9 August 1933 leaving Mary with nine children; the youngest just four years old.

The 1930s were particularly difficult years for farmers in Ireland. Eamon De Valera and the Fianna Fail Government withheld the payment of land annuities from Ireland to the British Government in June 1932, resulting in the "economic war" with Britain which was to continue until 1938. There was no export sale for cattle or other farm produce, making the 1930s a decade of poverty and hunger for the Irish people.

Because of her husband's early membership of the Royal Irish Constabulary (RIC) in the 1920s, Mary Breen was perceived as a supporter of the "Blue Shirts" a National Guard set up in 1933 by the dismissed Chief Commissioner of the Garda Siochana, Eoin O'Duffy. Its distinctive dress caused the organisation to be known as "The Blue Shirts". In the year of its foundation it was proclaimed an unlawful association. Mary Breen's home was targetted by Sinn Fein, who sought to intimidate her.

The Breen's old homestead at Ballydonegan

Steam threshing

She was a survivor however and wasted nothing of her resources. Because of her husband's ill-health she was used to making decisions and was almost entirely self-sufficient; having home-produced wheatmeal, bread, jam, butter, milk, bacon, vegetables, apples and rhubarb. She was known to be "as tight as tuppence" in her management of money and all domestic stocks were kept under lock and key and measured out carefully.

Each week Mary Breen went to market in Enniscorthy with her butter and eggs for sale and with the money she got for them she purchased tea, sugar and soap powder, her only requirements. Whenever there was extra profit she bought a suit length and was known to have up to twenty suit-lengths in the house at any one time, in readiness for the necessity of any of her sons to have a new suit.

Money was always scarce, therefore in order to generate an income she undertook contract threshing with a steam engine, mill and pitcher and had three such threshing sets operating in the early 1940s. During the winter-feeding season the steam engine was used to drive a roller and plate mill to grind corn for feed for the neighbouring farmers.

In 1944, the business premises of her cousin Owen Keogh, Raheenduff came on the market for auction. It consisted of a grocery shop and bar, corn business, coal and manure. Mary attended the auction to see what price it would fetch. There was no bid at the auction and after a conversation with the auctioneer and her cousin a deal was struck making Mary Breen the new owner at a cost of £6,000 with a couple of years to pay it off.

The sign "Mary Breen & Sons" was placed over the door. Three of her sons Peter, Tom and John, were put into the business and within a short time, up to twenty people were employed as clerks in the shop, lorry drivers, threshing machine operators and on the farm. Mary Breen was the "major domo" of the business and remained so until her death.

In 1948 she bought a one hundred acre farm at Ballincash and in 1954 another farm of eighty acres at Garrynew. She had previously purchased contracting plant and set up two sons, Martin and Nick in the business of land drainage, which was an important feature of Irish agriculture in the 1950s. The land at Garrynew was extremely wet and unprofitable and consequently was obtained at a reasonable price. The Breens completely drained the land turning the farm into prime quality land.

In 1957 Mary Breen & Sons bought 279 acres of land at Clone for £12,000. The price was considered to be extremely high for that time and was said to have become "the talk of Wexford, Wicklow and Carlow". With her usual shrewdness, the purchase was opportune since the price of land soared within a short time of the purchase and the farm turned out to be a great bargain.

Her only extravagance was in dress. She believed in dressing herself and her family in the best she could afford and the only time she didn't question a price was when she bought an outfit for herself.

Her greatest achievement was that in spite of hardship and widowhood she was able to keep her family around her in County Wexford and successfully establish them in farming and business.

Mary Breen died on 20 February 1965 and is interred at Monageer.

Source: Breen family

Mercedes Bolger (1894-1980)

Musician - Philanthropist

Mercedes Bolger made Gorey her home when she married David J Bolger of John Bolger & Co. General Merchants, Gorey and Ferns.

She was the daughter of Sir Joseph McGrath, Registrar of the Royal University Dublin and Eleanor McAllister. The McGrath Family were Dublin tea importers. She had one brother, Fr Fergal McGrath SJ (one time President of Clongowes Wood College) and one sister Alice who married Gerard Kane Smith, Little Moyle, Co. Carlow.

She was educated in the Convent of The Sacred Heart Society, Mount Anville Dublin and Our Lady of Zion, London. A noted linguist she spoke German, Italian and French fluently. She specialised in music and studied violin in Dresden, Germany. She was also an accomplished player of the piano, cello, viola and the Irish harp. She was awarded a Bachelor of Music degree by the old Royal University, Dublin (now UCD) and taught in the Royal Irish Academy of Music up to the time of her marriage.

She developed a tremendous interest in the Irish harp and became a member of *Cairde na Cruite* (Friends of the harp). She worked zealously for the preservation and promotion of the Irish harp and its music and was noted for her musical arrangements for that instrument.

The Bolgers had five children; Ann, Mercedes, John, Mary and David. One of her daughters, Mercedes Garvey became an internationally known harpist.

Mercedes senior was a council member of the Music Association of Ireland and Foras Eireann; groups responsible for organising music recitals throughout the country. She was a founder member of Gorey Music Club and its Honorary Secretary for many years and conducted the orchestra for all Gorey Operatic Society productions in the 1920s and 1930s.

*Mercedes Bolger (2nd from rt) on the occasion of a visit by
President Sean T. O'Kelly and Mrs Phyllis O'Kelly to Loreto Abbey, Gorey in 1946*

On the outbreak of World War II, Mercedes Bolger threw herself actively into the work of the Irish Red Cross Society and was area Director of the county Wexford Branch and a founder member of the Gorey Branch where she served in various capacities including Branch Chairman. Under the auspices of the Irish Red Cross Society she was also responsible for launching the first Water Safety weeks in County Wexford in the late 1940s.

When World War II ended she organised the care of wartime refugees in the county; some of whom were accommodated at Mount St Benedict near Gorey. She was also actively involved in a number of other charitable organisations including the National Council for the Blind, The Irish Society for the Prevention of Cruelty to Children, the old Gorey Nursing Association and the Penny Dinners.

She was closely identified with many church-related organisations in Gorey and district including the Gorey Apostolic Work Society and was a founder member of the first Ferns Diocesan Pilgrimage to Lourdes in 1954. Becoming the Pilgrim's Chief Handmaid she supervised the volunteer women helpers who cared for invalids on the pilgrimages.

Her outdoor pursuits included fox-hunting and in her younger days she rode to hounds with the Island Hunt. She was a keen gardener and won many prizes in agricultural and horticultural shows.

She was a founder member of the ladies section of Courtown Golf Club and was Lady President of the Club for more than twenty years.

She died on 26 December, 1980 aged 86 years and is interred in Ferns cemetery.

Source: *The Guardian* 31/12/1980

Kathleen Browne c1916

A VERSE IN YOLA

Cham goeen to tell thee oa tuale at is drue
Ar is in Rosslaare oa mydhe goude and drue
Shoo wearth in her hate oa ribbone at is blue
And shoo goeth to ee Faythe earcha deu too

I'm going to tell you a tale that is true
There is in Rosslare a maid good and true
She wears in her hat a ribbon that is blue
And she goes to the Faythe every day too

Kathleen A Browne (1878-1943)

Known as a revolutionary, senator and historian, Kathleen Browne devoted her life to Ireland and all things Irish. She was born in 1878 at Rathronan Castle. Her mother was Mary Stafford of Baldwinstown Castle and her father was Michael Browne, Bridgetown, a member of a quintessential Catholic big farm family who had managed to regain control and ownership of some of their ancestral lands which had been confiscated during the Cromwellian settlement. Her father, who conducted an extensive grocery and hardware business in Bridgetown, took a prominent part in local, public and national affairs and was the organiser of the '98 centenary commemorations in County Wexford.

Kathleen was educated at Bridgetown National School and secondary school in Wexford town. Commitment to Catholicism and stress on education were notable characteristics of the Brownes.

Intensely interested in all things Gaelic, she was secretary of the Wexford branch of the Gaelic League and became involved with the Irish Volunteers in the 1914-22 period. She became a member of Sinn Fein and for fifteen years was prominently associated with the work of Arthur Griffith.

After flying a tricolour from the roof of Rathronan Castle during the 1916 Easter Rising, she attempted to get to the GPO in Dublin. Accompanied by Nell Ryan, they were arrested near Bray and jailed in Kilmainham. She was a close friend of Nell Ryan, Tomcoole, until during the civil war Kathleen sided with the Free State while Nell remained Republican and the two friends never spoke to each other again.

Kathleen's correspondence with Arthur Griffith, Thomas MacDonagh and Kate Ryan and her correspondence while in Kilmainham and Mountjoy in May and June 1916 have yet to be published.

She was a member of Seanad Eireann from 1929 to 1938 and was at that time a prominent member of Cumann na nGaedhal. On the formation of the Blue Shirts by General O'Duffy she joined that organisation and was conspicuous in the Senate for the constant wearing of a blue blouse.

*Kathleen Browne's certificate of membership of
Ladies Irish National Land League*

She has been described as "a hard, uncompromising, dogged individual" who alienated many with whom she came in contact. However she was an acknowledged authority on Wexford history and in 1927 published a history of Wexford which became a text book for senior pupils in National schools. In it she took the view that prior to the 1798 Insurrection, William Pitt, the British Prime Minister, planned the Union and needed an excuse to bring about that measure.

Kathleen Browne was a practical farmer, successfully managing a large mixed farm. She was a member of the Irish Farmers' Union and a founding member of both the Ui Cinnsealaigh Historical Society, and the South Leinster Branch of the Royal Society of Antiquaries of Ireland. Her work on other committees included the

Society for the Preservation of the Memorials of the Dead, Loch Garman Co-operative Society, the County Library Advisory Committee and Ancient Monuments Committee. She was the moving spirit, in 1938, in the preservation of the Great Saltee island as a bird sanctuary. [1]

An expert in the Yola dialect, she wrote what is believed to be the last letter written in it. An article by her entitled *The Ancient Dialect of the Baronies of Forth and Bargy, County Wexford* was published in the *1927 Journal of the Royal Society of Antiquaries of Ireland*. [2] She also contributed a number of articles to *An Cosantoir* and her last publication around 1940 is entitled *Was Wexford Betrayed to Cromwell - The Truth*.

Kathleen Browne died in 1943 aged 65 and is interred in the family plot at Mayglass.

Sources:
Bernard Browne
Kilmore Parish Journal no. 24, 1995-96.
(1) Kevin Whelan ed. , *Wexford History and Society,* Geography Publications Dublin (1987) pp485/7

(2) Royal Society Antiquaries of Ireland, Journal 97, (1927) pp127-37.

Mother Visitation Clancy (1842-1889)

Bridget Teresa Clancy (1842-1889)

Sister Visitation

In the dentist's waiting room, the possibility of a "Foundation of Nursing Sisters" for the Diocese of Ferns was explored and Bridget, who was not entirely happy with the exclusiveness of her Order, the Bon Secours' mission to the wealthier classes, agreed to fill the need for assistance of the sick and needy in the Diocese of Ferns.

She became a Wexford woman by adoption. Her father was Edward Clancy, a small tenant farmer, in Fermoyle, Ballyouskill, County Laois where she was born on 12 September 1842. At twenty-one years of age she entered the Sisters of the Bon Secours Order on 20 July 1863. This was a French Order of nuns which had established a convent in Mount Street Dublin.

A chance meeting with Bishop Thomas Furlong, Ferns (1859-1875) in 1871, while in a dentist's waiting room, was the first milestone in the establishment of a new religious Order; the Sisters of Saint John of God, whose mother-house was to be in Wexford town. Bridget Clancy had previously met the Bishop at the residence of a man named Doyle in Maudlintown, Wexford, where she had been sent to nurse the old gentleman. Bishop Furlong was a frequent visitor to the house and was much impressed by the young nun's dedication.

On 7 October 1871 the first sisters arrived in Wexford. These were Sisters M Philip Barron, M Kevin Byrne, M Joseph Costello, M Aloysius Grey and her sibling M Stanislaus Grey. Initially the Sisters of Mercy gave them accommodation in rooms in their convent at Summer Hill. On 25 October, they moved into a little cottage at Sallyville which the Bishop had procured for them. The cottage had no contents; not even a bed or a chair. The sisters had one shilling and sixpence between them. The Sisters of Mercy donated some beds, bed-linen and chairs and the Sisters of Adoration gave a deal table.

The new Congregation, was initially known as the Infirmarian Sisters, and became the pioneer sisters of the future St. John of God Order.

Desert Hospital near Kalgoorlie

It was not an auspicious beginning for the Order or for Bridget Clancy, who in 1872 had returned from France where she had been sent by the Bon Secours Order. She had taken the name of Sister Visitation in religion. The sisters set about nursing the sick poor in their homes. From there they went on to the workhouses. They were moved by the terrible poverty and living conditions they met in Wexford.

In 1871 Ireland was a poor country for the majority of the people. The demand for Home Rule had begun in 1870 but was not in fact achieved. Families were large and it was common for families to have ten or more children although infant mortality was high.

In 1873 Sister Visitation applied for the post of head nurse in Wexford's workhouse hospital. She was successful and two sisters took up duty there. At the request of the Governors, two sisters also took up duty in the Houghton hospital New Ross. Another new departure was the opening of St. Joseph's Home for poor and homeless women in a house in Hill Street Wexford on 21 November 1874. The following year three sisters were sent to take charge of Enniscorthy workhouse and at the same time the Order was entrusted with schools in The Faythe.

Sallyville - the original home of The Institute of Sisters of St John of God

The work of the Sisters of Saint John of God also spread to other Dioceses. In Ossory, Waterford and Lismore and elsewhere the sisters dedicated themselves to nursing the sick in their homes, in the workhouses and fever hospitals; putting their own lives at risk in the interest of the patients.

During the gold rush of the 1890s in Australia, bad housing, polluted water and tainted food caused endemic fever outbreaks. Cavan-born Bishop Gibney of Perth wrote seeking help from the Saint John of God sisters in Wexford. A typhoid epidemic had taken many lives over the previous summer. Eight sisters who had been formed in the Novitiate in Wexford, took up the challenge and on the 16 October 1895 sailed on the *Orizaba* arriving in Albany on the 23 November. These were Sisters M John Gleeson, Celia Dunne, Antonio O'Brien, Ita Gleeson, Assumpta Hanley, Angela Brennan, Bridget O'Hanlon and Magdalen Kenny. Within a short time Sister Bridget O'Hanlon died of typhoid but with typical courage and dedication the other seven carried on the work.

When the great gold strike was made at Kalgoorlie, two sisters followed the miners more than 300 miles across the open desert, along bush tracks, under a blistering sun to the canvas town of 200 miners, where disease raged. They began their work by attending the sick where they found them but within two years had procured a hospital, a school and a convent. The small congregation which had its roots in Wexford had arrived in Australia. Re-inforcements were sent from Wexford and at Perth, the sisters took charge of a large and growing hospital. The work of the sisters of Saint John of God was acknowledged in the centenary year of 1995 when their pioneering work in establishing Australia's first hospital service was commemorated.

In Wexford, under Bridget's leadership they undertook nursing and education and established the Congregation which would become known world-wide as the Institute of Sisters of St. John of God. A central novitiate for Ireland was established in Wexford on 16 October 1924. The Generalate of the Order to-day is in Wexford town. The original home of the Order, Sallyville Cottage is still in use as a sisters' residence.

In 1944, Ely House Wexford was purchased and opened as a private hospital by the sisters and in 1947 Parkton House Enniscorthy was purchased and opened by them as a private nursing home.

Sister Visitation Clancy died of Tuberculosis, in the convent at Wexford, on 29 October 1889 at the age of 47. She had said: "Everyone is made of his day, what he does is not the work of any other day, but of his own day; his work is necessary. . . as a stepping stone on which we who come next are to raise our own work".

Bridget Clancy's legacy is apparent in missions in England, Rome, Pakistan, Africa and in Australia where leprosy was widespread among the Aboriginal peoples. It continues in the lives and work of the sisters of Saint John of God; women who believe that "only in love for the living is the spirit praised. . . ".

To-day the Saint John of God congregation is divided into two provinces - Saint Patrick's Province which has 302 locations in Ireland, two in England, one in Wales, one in Rome, one in Cameroon and Saint Therese's Province which has many houses and hospitals in Australia and Pakistan. The sisters went to Nigeria in 1960, setting up secondary schools and hospitals, until forced to leave during the Biafran War.

One sister closer to home, was the well-remembered Sister Philip Kelly who ministered to the sick and needy of the town of Wexford in their own homes for forty-five years up to the time of her death in 1978.

Born in Colga, Enniskeen, County Monaghan, in 1896, she arrived in Wexford at the age of twenty-six to enter the Novitiate of the Saint John of God Order where she took her final vows in 1926. She had already qualified as a nurse at the Mater Hospital Belfast.

She was known in almost every household in the town and became a legend in her own lifetime gaining for herself the soubriquet "The Florence Nightingale of Wexford". In an era when state social services and free hospitalisation were unheard of, she worked seven days a week in all weathers and her courage and dedication were legendary. She did not confine her services to any one section of the community but served all.

She retired at seventy-five years of age and was awarded the Papal *Bene Merenti* Medal for her outstanding service.

She died on 30 October 1978 aged eighty-two and is interred in the cemetery attached to the Saint John of God Convent Wexford.

The story of Bridget Clancy and the Saint John of God Order is told in *To Speed on Angels' Wings* by John Scally which was published in 1995 to celebrate a centenary of service by the Saint John of God Order in Australia.

Sources:
Sisters M Eugenie Brennan and Anne Harpur of the Institute of Sisters of Saint John of God.
The People (Wexford)20/10/1978

Mary Codd
Organist, Pianist, Painter

Mary Codd (1890-1964)

Musician

Always referred to as Miss Codd, her name was synonymous with music in Wexford town. She was born at Fisher's Row Wexford in 1890, daughter of one of Wexford's old schooner captains. She had one brother; the Very Rev. John Canon Codd, Parish Priest of Ferns.

The Codd family were among the first Anglo-Saxons who came to Ireland with Robert Fitzstephens and settled in Forth and Bargy soon after 1169. Rathaspeck Castle was erected by the Codds in 1351 and in 1346 Roger Codd was Abbot of Tintern.

Mary Codd was educated at Loreto Abbey Gorey where she was a classmate of Phyllis Ryan, who later became wife of President Sean T O'Kelly. In her early years she showed a keen interest in and love of music. She won high honours as a pianist and became a Licentiate of London College of Music. She taught music and directed the training of choirs in the various schools in Wexford along with training private pupils. She took a keen interest in boys and girls whose voices showed promise and her pupils and choirs won numerous awards at Feiseanna. Many local outstanding singers and musicians were numbered among her pupils.

She was Director of the Parish Choirs and organist in the Parish Churches for thirty-two years and during that time rarely failed to take her place at the organ during church ceremonies. She played a major part in the development of Gregorian Chant in Wexford. During her annual vacation she regularly attended either refresher courses or set herself to study some new facet of composition or modern trend in training methods.

In 1961 she received from Pope John XXIII the *Bene merenti* gold medal and an inscribed scroll for her work for the church.

Mary Codd was also a talented painter and wood-carver and being a kinswoman of Thomas Moore, whose mother was Anastatia Codd, she showed poetic ability. In fact it was the combination of "fine arts" that put the stamp of distinction on all her work.

She was associated with the Gaelic League from its earliest days and did great service to Irish music, language and culture. She seldom failed to include a number of Irish songs in her programmes for choral festivals.

Mary Codd fostered a love of music in Wexford town which became the well-spring from which the Wexford Festival of Music and the Arts flowed. In 1951 prominent members of Wexford Gramophone Society, including Doctor Tom Walshe, Seamus O'Dwyer, (the singing postman) Doctor Desmond Ffrench and Eugene McCarthy dreamed of bringing live performances to Wexford.

From modest beginnings to International status Wexford gave a lead to the country as a whole because nowhere else in Ireland had they anything quite like the Wexford Festival which has won the admiration and acclaim of lovers of opera world-wide.

Although the demands on her spare time were many, Mary Codd gave her time generously to voluntary effort and was conductor and musical director for light operas and pantomimes presented by local groups without pecuniary gain. She often attended six functions in one day; five of them in the churches.

She was a founder member of Wexford String Orchestra and it was while conducting the opening item of a Gaelic League Concert in Dun Mhuire that she collapsed and was taken to hospital where she died at 7 am next morning.

Mary Codd died on 16 March 1964 and is interred in Saint Ibar's cemetery Crosstown.

Sources:
The People (Wexford) 10/10/1959, 20/3/1964

Máire Comerford (1893-1982)

Republican

Máire Comerford was a direct descendant of Sir Geoffrey Esmonde of Huntingdon, in Lincolnshire. Sir Geoffrey was among the thirty Norman knights with names like Synott, Roche, Furlong, Meyler, Brown, Stafford and Walshe who landed at Bannow in 1169. Ballinastragh, near Gorey, became the seat of the Esmondes and Máire was a daughter of Mary Eva Esmonde of Ballinastragh and James Comerford, owner of Rathdrum Mills.

The Esmondes were sincerely Catholic but being land owners under the Crown they were conscious of an obligation of loyalty to the Crown of England and in the chequered history of Ireland often found themselves with the dilemma of divided loyalties.

Máire's first job was as secretary to the historian, Alice Stopford Green in whose home she met, among others, Michael Collins, Arthur Griffith, Jack Yeats and Maud Gonne. In her early twenties she visited friends in Dublin during Easter week 1916 and saw a detachment of the Citizen Army marching to the city centre. She knew little of the rising tide of nationalism but in the months after the surrender and execution of the leaders of the Rising she learned the essentials of Republicanism and began a life-long devotion to propaganda in its name.

On New Year's Day 1921, she was arrested and spent four months in the North Dublin Union Internment Camp, from which she escaped. She was re-captured in June and imprisoned in Kilmainham where she went on hunger strike. On her twenty-seventh day of hunger strike she was released from prison.

As a member of Cumann na mBan, the jobs assigned to Máire Comerford included travelling, organisation and intelligence work as well as fund-raising throughout the country for the Irish White Cross, a relief organisation for prisoners and dependents. She was, for a time during the "troubles", driver for Erskine Childers .

Máire Comerford - Veteran Republican, c1980

The events of the Civil War, one of which was the burning of Ballinastragh House by Anti-Treaty Forces, discouraged and depressed Máire Comerford and she spent ten years out of work and politics. During this period Reverend Dom Sweetman of Mount Saint Benedict provided a refuge for her and she remained one of his most loyal supporters in controversial circumstances. In the 1920s, Máire and her mother ran a school for girls in Courtown along the lines of the school for boys run by Father Sweetman at Mount Saint Benedict.

In 1953 she joined the Irish Press; writing for the Woman's Page and remained in employment there until her retirement at an advanced age. In the introduction to her book *The First Dáil* published in 1969, she says:

> I am indebted for their wisdom, their courage, their great experience and their interest in the youth fifty years ago, when it was sheer joy to us to be alive and taking part in a fight for Ireland and justice, shoulder to shoulder with our own at ground level, to such men and women as Rev. John Francis Sweetman OSB, Alice Stopford Green, Gobnait Ni Bruadair, Aine Ceannt, Sean Etchingham, Charlie Murphy, Hannah Sheehy-Skeffington.

> Then there were the families who accepted me into comradeship; the Woods, the Humphreys, the Plunketts, the Phelans, the O'Donnells, the Barrys. This was only one segment of the great chain of friendships which extended at home and abroad, wherever the Irish were in revolt.

Máire Comerford was not an ardent feminist. She fought for the National Movement and for the fulfilment of the republican promises of the First Dáil. She believed that women were kept out of real power, being in the relief organisations, although as she herself put it "some of them were more able than the men and they knew it".

Máire Comerford died on 15 December 1982 and according to her wishes, her remains were laid beside those of Father Dom Sweetman and Miss Aileen Keogh at Mount Saint Benedict; the site of the Benedictine school founded by Father Sweetman and formerly Mount Nebo, the home of the infamous magistrate Hunter Gowan of 1798. In her long life time she had earned for herself the soubriquet "the grand old dame of republicanism".

Sources:
Owen Esmonde - Esmonde Family Tree
The Link, vol 15 No. 2 Whit 1989

Mother Patrick Cosgrave c1882

Mary Anne Cosgrave (1863-1900)

Known as Mother Patrick, Mary Anne Cosgrave was the first white woman to visit Rhodesia, now Zimbabwe and managed to pack a lifetime of distinguished service into her short lifespan before her death at the early age of thirty-seven. She was the daughter of James Cosgrave of Ballysillagh, Oylegate, a member of the Royal Irish Constabulary (RIC) and Mary Rochford. The Cosgraves had four sons Peter, James, William and John and two daughters Mary Anne and Catherine.

Mary Anne was born on 22 May 1863 at Summerhill, near Trim while her father was serving in County Meath. Both parents contracted tuberculosis and died within a year of each other; James on 6 November 1869 and Mary on 1 November 1870. It is believed that two sons Peter and John also died young from tuberculosis while William and James grew up and found work on the Dublin-Wexford railways.

The two little girls Mary Anne, then seven years old and Catherine aged five, were taken and reared by John Cosgrave, Ballinavary, Davidstown about six miles outside Enniscorthy. They received their early education at Davidstown National School and later attended Loreto Convent secondary school in Enniscorthy as day pupils.

Mary Anne was noted as a gentle good girl although not a great student. She left school at fifteen years of age and worked as an assistant in a drapery shop in Wexford town.

When Bishop JD Ricards of Eastern Cape, South Africa came to Wexford to seek vocations to the priesthood and sisterhood in his diocese, Mary Anne decided that this was where her future lay and with a party of young priests and postulants she sailed for Cape Town in 1880. On 19 January 1881, she entered the convent of the Dominican Sisters in King Williams Town and a year later made her profession; taking Sister Mary Patrick as her name in religion.

The Cosgrave homestead at Ballinavarry

Perceived to have a natural talent for teaching Sister Patrick taught in various convents in the Cape area of South Africa including King Williams Town, East London and Potchefstroom until 1890.

In 1890 feeling herself called to nurse the sick, she volunteered for work which was was to lead to her fame as a courageous pioneer. The previous year, an Englishman named Cecil Rhodes, a member of the Cape Assembly who had made a fortune in the diamond mines of Kimberley, had formed a British Chartered Company. He sought concessions from a native king, Lobengula, for British trading and mining in Matabeleland. Dr Jameson, a friend of Rhodes who had settled in practice in Kimberely, had used his influence over his royal patient and in 1889, Lobengula had granted a charter to the British South Africa Company. The following year an expeditionary force set out on that long and dangerous trek to Matabeleland and the adjoining Mashonaland.

On hearing that the Zambezi Mission territory was being opened up by Father Daignault SJ who sought assistance from the Dominican Sisters in King Williams Town, Sister Patrick volunteered to go there. She was chosen to be in charge of a small

5/5: We started for Maclouche on the 5th of May & without any break in the monotony of our journey we
came in sight of the Camp on the 10th of May. Saturday
evening. As our oxen neared the Camp, the men
formed into two lines for our waggons to pass
through and burst forth into a bold & prolonged
cheer, which had the effect of frightening the oxen,
and causing them to get entangled in the yokes. We
were obliged to get out & walk thro' the two lines of
men to the Hospital. They continued their cheering
and showed by every sign how grateful they were
to us for coming up to take care of them. It was
dark when we got to our destination, still a tent was
soon pitched in which we had tea & read the bundle
of letters which were waiting for us & which Mr Slater
was kind enough to bring us at once on our arrival.

A page from Mother Patrick's diary

group of five Sisters who were selected to nurse the pioneer column on their way north.

On 22 February 1890 they arrived at the Jesuit Mission station at Mafeking and nursed the sick there for seven weeks until 13 April when, accompanied by Father Prestage, as chaplin, the Sisters set out on their 400 mile journey north. Mother Patrick wrote an account of the journey in her diary:

> An enormous ox-wagon was hired which was to be our abode for the next five weeks. We viewed this kind of conveyance with mixed feelings and our apprehension grew when we were told that it was to be pulled by a span of sixteen oxen. The departure was fixed for 4 o'clock when the oxen would be sure to be on the spot ready for the journey to begin. 4 o'clock came and went, so did 5 o'clock and 6 o'clock, but no oxen made their appearance. We had received a note saying that we had better sleep in the wagon for our span of oxen was lost and if found might be inspanned (yoked) when the moon rose. When we awoke in the morning we had not moved from the spot.

A further entry in her diary on 28 April 1890 stated:

> We came to an open space and here, close to the Limpopo or Crocodile River, the oxen were unyoked. Our habits and other apparel were in dire need of soap and water and in a short time a curious procession armed with buckets and other implements wended its way to the banks of the river. One of the drivers joined the procession cracking his big whip to scare away the crocodiles. Hippopotami tracks along the river, the unearthly laugh of the hyena, the fierce bark of the jackal and the dismal howling of the baboons made us realise that we were in the heart of the African wilderness.

The diaries of Mother Patrick graphically describe their experiences on the journey and were later published in a book entitled *In God's White Robed Army - a Chronicle of the Dominican Sisters in Rhodesia.*

On 10 May the sisters arrived at Macloutsie where they were greeted with a guard of honour and loud and prolonged cheering with the result that the oxen took fright and got entangled in the yokes.

Next day a marquee was pitched to serve as a chapel and two marquees and four bell-tents served as a hospital for twenty-seven patients, who up to this were lying on the ground with nothing but their blankets and waterproof sheets to cover them. Later an iron house with a thatch roof replaced the hospital tents and it was visited by the Governor of the Colony, Lord Elphinstone.

Cecil Rhodes also visited the hospital and ordered that huts be built for the nuns to replace the tents in which they lived. There are many references in *Mother Patrick and her Nursing Sisters* by Michael Gelfand to Rhodes' interest in the work of the sisters and the fact that he was "very pleased in the Sisters work. . . asks that whenever anything is wanted we should let him know".

After a ten month stay in Macloutsie the pioneer Sisters set out, for Fort Tuli, on the next stage of their journey, leaving replacement Sisters in Macloutsie. The rains were particularly heavy that year and there were many cases of malaria fever and dysentery. The Sisters set up a primitive hospital and plodded from tent to tent, ankle deep in mud, in the pelting rain, to care for the sick.

On 5 June 1891 Mother Patrick and her little group set out on the final leg of their journey to Salisbury (Harare). It proved to be a difficult one "as the wagon kept sticking in the wet ground and swamps". At last on 27 July they arrived in Salisbury and began their work on improving the hospital which consisted of three large huts, a marquee and some tents, all of which showed signs of sad neglect.

The place was soon transformed but it was necessary to arm the patients with sticks to beat off the rats as rat bites and snake poisoning were common ailments. The natives, never having seen a white woman before, sat for hours on end, with arms folded, staring at the Sisters; who were the first white women to visit that part of the world.

On 18 October 1892, a wattle and daub school was opened in Salisbury and ten scholars began their lessons in what was Rhodesia's first school. Outbreaks of fever and small pox were endemic and the Sisters did not escape recurrent attacks.

In 1896 when rebellion broke out among the Matabele tribe a force called the "Rhodesia horse" was equipped to go to the help of

Detail from National Tapestry of Rhodesia

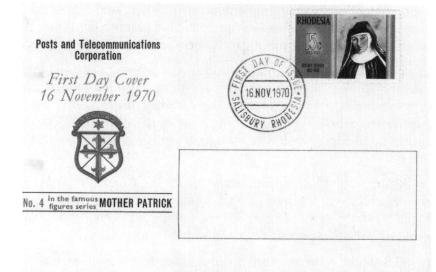

Posts and Telecommunications
Corporation

First Day Cover
16 November 1970

No. 4 in the famous figures series **MOTHER PATRICK**

RHODESIA
15c

FIRST DAY OF ISSUE
16.NOV.1970
SALISBURY RHODESIA

Commemorative Stamp in honour or Mother Patrick

the colonists in Gwelo. The Sisters were asked to join the column and suffered many privations. Owing to a cattle disease there was neither meat, milk nor butter and they had to depend on whatever tinned foods were available. When the rebellion was crushed the sisters returned to Salisbury.

By 1898 the Dominicans had established a nursing community in Fort Victoria (1892) a nursing and teaching community in Bulawayo (1894) and a community for missionary work in Chishawasha Mission (1898) along with the hospital and school in Salisbury.

Mother Patrick was elected Prioress of the Rhodesian community. In 1898 she was awarded the Royal Order of the Red Cross by Queen Victoria in recognition of her heroic work. She was invited to Windsor Castle but declined to travel.

She returned to Ireland in search of postulants and took the opportunity, while in Dublin, to qualify for a Matron's certificate in nursing. During her stay in Ireland she travelled to Wexford for a few days in order to receive visits from her relations and old friends. By this time Mother Patrick was already ill with tuberculosis. She wrote:

> The most trying part of the visit to Wexford was the going to see dear old Aunt Mary and Uncle Gaby. . . . The drive to me was of course full of memories which all came back with full force. . . he was the first to meet us and I never saw anyone so much affected. He could not speak at all and the tears fell from his eyes. . . No use describing the five hours we spent there, you can imagine it.

However she returned to Rhodesia, arriving back in Salisbury in December 1898, with six postulants she had recruited while in Ireland. Her health, due to repeated bouts of fever, continued to decline, until after a particularly serious turn she died on 31 July 1900.

On the day of her funeral every store in Salisbury was closed as a mark of respect. Flags flew at half mast and practically the whole town attended at the graveside. There was an immense funeral cortege and Cecil Rhodes was among the chief mourners.

Three years after her death a Celtic Cross was erected on her grave and this was unveiled on Saint Patrick's Day 1903, by the Irish

Mashonaland Association. There is an annual pilgrimage to Mother Patrick's grave in Mashonaland (now Zimbabwe) where her memory is still revered. The ecumenical nature of her work was recognised by a memorial plaque in the Anglican Church in Salisbury and also a memorial to her in the Salisbury Catholic Cathedral. In 1970, a stamp was issued by the Rhodesian Government to commemorate this famous lady of County Wexford.

In the House of Parliament, which faces onto Cecil Square Salisbury, the history of Rhodesia, in needlework, comprised of 42 embroidered panels worked by the Women's Institutes of Rhodesia and known as The National Tapestry, occupies three walls of the dining hall. The panels measure 100ft by 17inches wide. One of the panels depicts Cecil Rhodes' visit to Mother Patrick and the four Dominican Sisters who worked with her.

The death of Mother Patrick in 1900 marked the end of the early pioneering period in South Africa.

All things by immortal power near or far
Hiddenly - to each other linked are
That thou canst not stir a flower
Without troubling a star   Francis Thompson

Sources:
Bernard Browne: *County Wexford Connections* (Wexford undated)
Doris Burton: *Heroic Nuns* (1965)
Des Byrne: "Mother Patrick - The first Irishwoman in Zimbabwe", *The Pioneer* (June 1991)
Nicholas Cosgrave: *Mother Patrick - Mary Anne Cosgrave 1863 - 1900,* (unpublished and undated)
AJ Dachs & WF Rea: *The Catholic Church and Zimbabwe 1879-1979,* (1980)
'Dominican Sister': *In God's white-robed army* (1947)
Michael Gelfand: *Mother Patrick & her nursing Sisters,* (1964)
Patrick Hennessey: "Mother Patrick Cosgrave 1863-1900" *Davidstown-Courtnacuddy Parish History* (1982)
Mashonaland Irish Association Centenary Year Booklet (1991)
Ferrara Weinzierl OP: *Mother Patrick - First Superior of the Dominican Sisters in the Zambezi Mission* (1991)
Ferrera Weinzierl OP: *100 Years Dominican Sisters in Zimbabwe 1891 - 1991*

(1991)

Madge Dixon and Mary Doyle

Two Wexford soldier women of the 1798 Insurrection

The women of 1798 had no part in the political process. They had no vote and could not hold property in their own right unless as widows they inherited from their husbands. Consequently there is very little in the records about the women of that period.

Nevertheless, although not in leadership roles, a great number of women took an active part in the Insurrection and fully supported the United Irish Society's ideals of liberty and equality; which, had they but known, did not apply to women.

Apart from the passive and caring roles played by the patriot women, women were active as providers of food for the insurgents. They acted as intelligence agents, spies and informers and many in active soldiering. Two active soldier women of Wexford in 1798 were Madge Dixon and Mary Doyle.

Margaret (Madge) Dixon was the wife of Thomas Dixon, son of a publican in Castlebridge, who was a sea-captain and also a captain in the United Irish Society. She accompanied her husband at all times throughout the 1798 Insurrection in Wexford. Sir Richard Musgrave in his *Memoirs* described her as "remarkable for the ferocity of her disposition". There exists the strange story of Madge Dixon, proceeding to the home of Colonel le Hunte at Artramont about four miles from Wexford. On discovering orange coloured furniture in the house she declared she had discovered where the Orangemen held their lodge. Taking an orange fire-screen from the le Hunte home and bearing it aloft she entered Wexford Town on horseback. There she attempted to raise a body of people to take Colonel le Hunte and have his blood. However he was reprieved due to the intervention of the local curate, Father Broe.

A more realistic light may have been shed on the malevolence of Madge Dixon by the Reverend Robert Leech of Drumlane Rectory Belturbet. In a letter published in *The People* on 13 August 1898, he tells that his wife's grandfather, who was taken with others by the Dixons, escaped death at Wexford Bridge by the intervention of Bishop James Caulfield. They escaped a second time by the intervention of Father John Corrin and a third time by the rapid advance of the soldiers. The letter continues:

> It is but right to say that from all I have been able to ascertain Dixon's wife, a tall fine-looking woman, had been previously outraged by one of the soldiers and this seems to have been the cause of their fury and revenge.

This may explain the reason for the vindictiveness of the Dixons who were particularly noted for their cruelty in '98.

There is no account of what happened finally to Captain Thomas Dixon and his wife Madge. George Taylor in his account of '98 states that "wherever they secreted themselves, they never could be found, though a large reward was offered for their apprehension".

Mary Doyle, Castleboro, stands out for her gallantry at the battle of New Ross in 1798. Nothing is known of her family background. She is recorded in PF Kavanagh's *A popular history of the Insurrection of 1798* as "An amazon named Doyle, who marched with the insurgent army and bore herself as gallantly as the most courageous man". She engaged herself in cutting off, with a bill-hook, the cross belts of the fallen dragoons and handing them together with the cartouche boxes to her comrades. She is remembered also for her insistence that a cannon held by the United Irishmen at New Ross be taken from the battle scene by the Insurgents.

There is no conclusive evidence as to what happened to Mary Doyle after the battle of Ross but it is thought that she perished in the flames that consumed much of New Ross at that time.

William Rooney wrote a romantic 36 line ballad entitled "The heroine of Ross" which includes a line "Let that maiden's name be cherished while the Barrow's waters flow" but neglects to mention anywhere in the ballad that her name was Mary Doyle.

Sources:
Richard Musgrave, *Memoirs of the Irish Rebellion of 1798*, ed. SW Myers and D McKnight (Indiana, 1995)
The People Wexford 13 August 1898
Charles Dickson, *The Wexford Rising in 1798* (Tralee 1956)
George Taylor, *Rebellion in Wexford in the Year 1798* (Dublin 1800)
P. F. Kavanagh, A popular history of the Insurrection of 1798 (1898)

Bronze 1798 memorial plaque designed and executed by St. Senan's Parents'
Group and reproduced here by kind permission of the group
Co-ordinator: Maeve McCauley, Artist-Facilitator: Paddy Darrigan
Kathleen Dobbs, Kathleen Doran, Edel Hogan, Edel Kinsella, Edel Cahill,
Patricia Hyland, Cathy Davin, Julie Moorhouse-O'Leary.

Margaret Fitzpatrick c1910

Margaret Fitzpatrick (c1850-1925)

Entrepreneur in Tourism

Margaret Fitzpatrick was the daughter of William Doyle, a small farmer in Clonegal on the Wexford-Carlow border. In 1870, she married seafarer John Fitzpatrick second son of James Fitzpatrick and Catherine Byrne, Riverchapel, kinsman of renowned Ship's-master Kate Tyrell Fitzpatrick of Arklow. Fitzpatrick's house on "The Banks" at Seamount, Courtown overlooked the sea and the new harbour built by the Earl of Courtown which was completed in 1847. Courtown with its wide sweep of bay had the natural resources to develop into a tourist resort.

The building of the harbour and subsequent growth of the village (1825-1860) ensured that it became a popular venue for day-trippers from the surrounding hinterland who wished to view the new harbour. Many of these put their pony-traps and carts into Fitzpatrick's yard; the ponies and horses were turned loose to graze in the adjoining field while "the bathers" enjoyed a day at the seaside.

At the end of the day, the visitors returned to Fitzpatricks with a keen appetite. Margaret Fitzpatrick saw the opportunity of reaping a new "harvest of the sea" and began a catering service. She charged sixpence for a "plain tea" which consisted of tea, bread, butter and jam and one shilling and sixpence for a "meat tea" which was a plate of cold slices of meat with tea, bread, butter and jam. She thus became the first person to offer a catering service in the resort and later opened the first guest house in Courtown Harbour.

The 1914-18 war in Europe was a boon to tourism in Courtown as those who had previously spent their holidays abroad could no longer do so. Margaret Fitzpatrick prospered and Courtown became a popular family resort. Today Courtown Harbour is the premier holiday resort on the south east coast.

Fitzpatricks had six sons, James, William, Andrew, Thomas who died young, John and another child called Thomas, all of whom

Kitty Fitzpatrick c1920

joined the Merchant Navy and also one daughter Catherine (Kitty) who helped Margaret run the catering business.

Kitty married Courtown's Harbour Master Denis Murphy, who was prominently associated with the movement for Irish Independence since the early days of the Irish Volunteers. He was a staunch supporter of all gaelic cultural and sporting organisations and was a close friend and colleague of Sean Etchingham, Minister for Agriculture and Fisheries in the first Sinn Fein Dail Eireann and was the only Courtown man to accompany Etchingham to Enniscorthy for the 1916 Rising.

Kitty became a prominent member of Cumann na mBan. During the critical years of the struggle for Independence her home was always open to those "on the run" and many people found a refuge there.

Throughout her life, she continued the catering business and saw the tourist trade in Courtown Harbour develop and change from self-catering rented rooms in the late 19th century, through full board, partial board, bed and breakfast, to the caravan/mobile home boom of the 1960s. She handed on a well established family business to a third generation who carried it on until 1989 when after more than a hundred years of involvement in the tourist trade the family retired.

Margaret Fitzpatrick died on 2 September 1925. Her daughter Kitty (Murphy) died on 3 April 1965; both are interred in Ardamine cemetery.

Sources:
The Guardian, 8 April 1965
Murphy family

Courtown Harbour c1900

Alice Furlong (1875-?)

Poet

Alice Furlong was the daughter of John Walter Furlong, Crandaniel, Barntown. She was born in Tallaght, County Dublin in 1875 and was sister-in-law of PJ McCall, author, poet and composer of the most popular '98 ballad; *Boolavogue.*

In 1899 she published a collection of poems entitled *Roses and Rue.* The book was dedicated to the memory of her dead mother. Her father met a sudden and tragic death in 1898 and her mother died within a short time of his death. In the same year her eldest sister Mary who was a writer and contributor to the *Irish Monthly* died of a fever contracted when nursing the poor at Roscommon Fever Hospital.

Along with her songs of mourning Alice Furlong wrote religious poems and lyrics full of the joy of life and the beauty of the world. In her poem "Trees" she wrote:

. . . Sunlight comes laughing through
And rain and honeyed dew
Scatter pale pearls at every green embrasure.

In 1907 Alice published *Tales of fairy folks, queens and heroes.* Her poem *Dublin Easter 1916* was published in that year and was followed in 1917 by the publication of *Two poems of triumph and death* in collaboration with Alice Milligan. Of these *The Dead Bishop* was composed by Alice Furlong and *Glasnevin* by Alice Milligan.

In 1918 *Comhradh Beirte* - Dialogues *as Gaeilge* (A collection of rhymed and consecutive phrases and idioms in common use) compiled by Alice Furlong, was published by the Talbot Press.

Sources:
Shan Van Vocht Vol. 1 No3 p1 M/F
Hayes Catalogue National Library of Ireland

Lily Parle (extreme right) represented Leinster in Interprovincial camogie in 1956, '57, '60, '62 and '63

Lily Furlong - née Parle (1934 - 1997)

In 1934 when hurling was considered to be a man's game, a camogie star was born at Kellystown, Drinagh on 6 March. She was the daughter of Nicholas Parle, county council road ganger and Mary Alice (nee Bail) dressmaker.

Lily Parle had one brother James, one step-brother Toddy Bail and one step-sister Mary Parle. She received her primary education at Piercestown National School and studied Domestic Science at Wexford Technical School. On leaving schools, she was employed in Fine Wool Fabrics at Kerlogue.

From an early age Lily showed an outstanding talent for hurling. She learned her skills in John Furlong's field at Kellystown where neighbouring boys and girls played hurling every evening when weather permitted. Instead of playing with hurleys, which the children could not always afford, hooked sticks (potsticks) cut from the ditches provided an excellent substitute.

In the 1950s camogie was promoted by a small number of pioneers including Jim Sinnott (Wexford), Nick Doyle (Broadway), Tom Dunne and his wife Margaret, Leo Carty and MJ Power.

Lily Parle became a key player for Saint John's Camogie Club. The first competition in which she participated was a seven-a-side in which Saint John's beat Saint Leonard's. With her club, Lily won five County Championship medals in the years 1954, '58, '60, '61, '62. Her inter-county career began in 1953.

For thirteen years, from 1953 to 1965, she played on the Wexford County Camogie team, captaining the team on numerous occasions. She captained Wexford to win four Leinster Intermediate medals in the years 1962-1965 inclusive; having been runners-up in 1959.

She represented Leinster in interprovincial camogie in 1956, '57, '60, '62 and '63; being at times the only Wexford player selected for Leinster.

She won two Interprovincial (Gael-Linn Cup) medals with Leinster; one in 1956 when she was the only Wexford representative on the Leinster team and the other in 1962 when she captained the team and had three Wexford colleagues. In 1962 Leinster defeated Ulster at Casement Park; securing the Interprovincial title.

In 1964 she won the John Power award for best camogie player and in the same year she married Sean Furlong a native of Kilmuckridge; a driver in the Library service of Wexford County Council. There were three children of the marriage; two sons John and Michael and a daughter Ann. In 1971 the Power's Gold Label Wexford Sports Star award for the outstanding player of the past was won by Lily Parle.

As chairperson of the County Wexford Camogie Board up to the time of her death Lily was remarkable for her encouragement to all young players particularly the Faythe Harriers' camogie team which she trained.

A Founder member of the children's crab-fishing contest which has been a successful part of the Wexford Opera Festival fringe events, Lily helped to organise the competition for thirty years.

Apart from her sporting activities she was devoutly religious and was an active member of Bride Street Parish council along with membership of the parents' council of both Saint John of God school, The Faythe and Christian Brothers' school committees.

When Lily died on 30 July 1997, camogie players from clubs throughout the county bore their jerseys on their shoulders in a guard of honour at her funeral and, as she was borne from the church the Wexford hurling anthem *The Purple and Gold* was sung by Theresa Kehoe.

She is interred in her native parish of Piercestown.

Sources:
Sean Furlong
Billy Quirke "Memories" No 165 The Echo, 1988,
Nicholas Furlong *The Echo* August 1997
George Bridges *The Echo* August 1997.

Maureen Golden (1910-1993)

Department of Agriculture Inspector of Poultry-keeping and Dairying

Maureen Golden was one of the pioneers of the agricultural advisory service in county Wexford in the 1930s. The daughter of Bridget Curtis, Knockduff, Bree and Maurice Golden, a commercial traveller, Maureen was born on 28 May 1910 in Tralee; A brother Frank was born on 12 May 1912 and one sister Winifred on 1 November 1914. After the birth of Winifred, Maureen and Frank were brought to Knockduff in November 1914 and were reared there by the maternal grandparents.

Maureen received her early education in Bree National School; her secondary education in the Mercy Convent, Enniscorthy and as a boarder in Loreto, Stephen's Green Dublin, where she became Head Girl.

In 1929 she attended the Rural School of Domestic Economy at Ramsgrange and later the Munster Institute where she qualified as an Instructor in Poultry-keeping and Dairying.

She was immediately employed by Drishane Convent to work and teach on their poultry farm. From there she was appointed by the newly formed County Wexford Committee of Agriculture as its first poultry advisor and took up duty in 1938. Her duties included:

Inspection of Poultry stations; Lectures; Investigation of hatching results obtained from eggs purchased at poultry stations; Taking of blood samples for baccillary white diarrhoea (BWD) from station holders' stock and stock owned by private breeders; Farm visitation to afford advice and assistance in disinfecting and setting up of incubators and rearers; Inspection of premises and selection of applicants for grants under the Committee of Agriculture schemes; Supervision of the erection of rearing houses and management of incubators; Selection of turkeys for stock purposes; Injection of turkeys for prevention of Blackhead; Culling farm flocks and preparation of poultry for table; Organisation of poultry sections of Enniscorthy and

Gorey Agricultural Shows; Selection of pullets for competition in the Egg-laying test conducted by the Department of Agriculture at the Munster Institute Cork.

The entire stock on all poultry stations was subjected to the blood test for BWD (bacillary white diarrhoea) and only birds showing a negative reaction to the test were selected as breeding stock, on the basis of body-size, health, stamina and breed. [1]

Maureen Golden was promoted to the position of Inspector in the Department of Agriculture. Her area was the south of Ireland where together with Frances Moran she worked on The Hatcheries Act 1947 and later, on the revised course for home management at the Munster Institute in 1962. [2]

On a personal level she was seen as a domineering, independent woman; always fashionably dressed and being among the first women to drive a car which she required for her work.

She retired in October 1976 and resided in Enniscorthy until her death at the age of 83. She died suddenly on 25 September 1993 and is interred at Enniscorthy.

Sources:
John Curtis
Frances Flynn
Alice Griffin, Department of Agriculture
(1) MT Connolly *Forty Years of Wexford Agriculture* (1996) p69
(2) Anna Day *More than one egg in the basket (The History of the Munster Institute* (1992) p140

Maureen Golden

Eileen Gray (1879-1976)

Interior designer and architect

Original pieces of Eileen Gray furniture are now highly prized by collectors and reproductions of her furniture, carpets and screens are being made to-day from her original designs. She was born on 8 August 1879, at Brownswood Manor near Enniscorthy. Her father was a member of a wealthy aristocratic, Scots-Irish family, long established in Enniscorthy and her mother was Baroness Eveleen Gray. She received her early education privately from governesses and later attended private schools in England and on the Continent. Having inherited an interest in painting from her father, an amateur artist, she went on to study art at the Slade School of Art in London and at the Academie Julian in Paris where she was one of the first women students. There she studied drawing and the fine arts and developed an intense interest in lacquer. She became apprenticed to Sugawara, a Japanese lacquer craftsman. Her initial interest in lacquered screens extended her attention to furniture, lamps and rugs.

In 1907 she settled in an apartment in Rue de Bonaparte, Paris, which she occupied until her death. In her early years flying and ballooning were among her interests and she accompanied Latham on an unsuccessful cross channel flight in 1909. In the early twenties she flew on the first airmail service in America from New Mexico to Acapulco. She served as an ambulance driver in France for a period during the early years of World War 1.

In 1911 she established her name as a professional designer of modernist furniture when she exhibited her work, which was made by her own craftsmen, at the Salon de la Societe des Artistes Decorateurs. The immediate years after the war involved her increasingly in the decorative arts and furnishings, resulting in the design of chairs.

In 1919 she opened a gallery, the Jean Desert, at 217 Faubourg Saint Honore, and won many prestigious commissions

Eileen Gray
Interior Designer
and Architect

to create entire environments for luxury apartments. In 1922, a room designed by Eileen Gray was exhibited at the *Union des Artistes Modernes*.

Having a natural talent for architecture, she was encouraged to try her hand by Jean Badovici, architect and co-editor of *l'Architecture Vivante* then a major propaganda organ of the new architecture. In 1926 she designed a house on a steeply sloping site on the Mediterranean which was called *Roquebrune* and was later occupied by Badovici. In 1929 details of the design were published in *l'Architecture Vivante*. The artist, Le Corbusier built his holiday cabin on an adjoining site and in the 1940s he painted five major murals in the Roquebrune house.

She designed her own house at Castellar and the use of *brise-soleil*, vertical slatted blinds, at both Roquebrune and Castellar, together with the rubble stone podium of the latter house became part of Corbusier's later work.

Samples of Eileen Gray's furniture designs

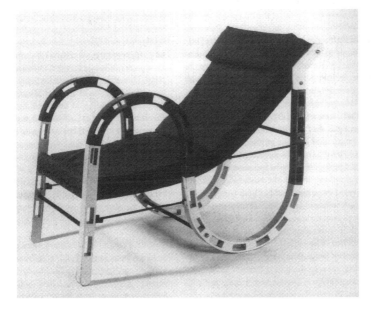

The house at Castellar was built as a holiday house for the owner and later became the home of Graham Sutherland. *Wendinegn*, a leading Dutch review, devoted an entire issue to the work of Eileen Gray in 1924.

In 1930-31, she designed a one-roomed flat in the rue Chateaubriand Paris. This demonstrated her concern for detail and materials and her ingenuity in maximising storage space by the use of a folding ladder to an overhead enclosure.

Outside an elite circle of contemporaries and patrons throughout her long life, Eileen Gray was largely unknown until 1972 when an auction of her work was held. Her talent was immediately recognised and she won many honours including Honorary Fellowship of the Royal Institute of Architects of Ireland in 1975.

Although her output was not large, the quality of her work has assured her a place among the contemporary masters of the Modern Movement of furniture design. Samples of her furniture may be seen at the Pompidou Centre, Paris and the Victoria and Albert Museum London.

She continues to influence to-days young architects and designers. In a recent interview (1998) Roisin Murphy, designer and co-presenter of RTE's interiors programme 'Beyond The Hall Door' mentioned that Eileen Gray, the county Wexford furniture designer had been the greatest influence on her work.

Eileen Gray died in her apartment on the Rue de Bonaparte Paris, on 31 October 1976. She is interred at Pere Lachaise cemetery in Paris.

Sources:
John Graby, Director RIAI, "The Architect and the Drawing" 1989 in RIAI's 150th Anniversary publication
James McQuillan; 1975 RIAI Yearbook
David Carbury and James Quirke, Enniscorthy Castle Museum Aidan Ryan

Elizabeth Hart (c1798-1863)

Emigrant

Elizabeth Hart was born at Ballymoney, Gorey, County Wexford c.1798. She was the only daughter of James (Larey) O'Leary who farmed at Ballymoney.

About 1825 she married Tom Hart of a family who came to Ireland from Kent, England in the late eighteenth century and who had started a tanyard in Watlin Square, Dublin. Hart was employed at different times as waterguard, lighthouse keeper and later, though not very successfully, in farming. The Harts had seven children; one son and six daughters. The son, who was the eldest, died at a very early age from whooping cough and, a few years later, three of the girls died in one week from the same disease.

About the year 1833, the Mexican Government sent two Texas - Irish empressarios, James Power and James Hewetson to Ireland with authority to introduce four hundred families in order to colonise a given territory within the Republic of Mexico.

Each family was to receive one league (3.456 statute miles) and one labor of land and every young man over eighteen years of age was to receive one quarter of a league. The Mexican Government agreed to furnish the head of each family with ten milch cows, one cart and a yoke of oxen also a garrison of soldiers to guard and protect the colonists against incursions of hostile Indians.

This seemed very attractive, since in early nineteenth century Ireland the majority of people lived in one-roomed cabins and existed mainly on potatoes. There were decades of famine before the great Famine of the 1840s.

Power, being a native of Ballygarrett arrived home about the beginning of June 1833. He posted handbills throughout the vicinity and adjoining counties and interested persons came to the home of his sister Elizabeth, who was married to Thomas O'Brien and lived near Ballygarrett.

In her old age, Elizabeth Hart's eldest daughter Bridget Rosalie (born c 1826) dictated to her granddaughter Mary Frances Priour Hatch, an autobiographical account of the tribulations of the Harts after leaving Wexford. The unpublished account was titled *The adventures of a family of emigrants who emigrated to Texas in 1834.*

Rosalie tells in her autobiography: "Colonel Powers held meetings at his sister's house and made speeches to large assemblies. He represented Texas as one of the richest countries in the world and having a most delightful climate. Gold was so plentiful, according to his account that you could pick it up under the trees".

Among the hundreds who decided to accompany him back to Texas were his sister Elizabeth, her husband Thomas and children, Mary, Brigid, Agnes, Andrew, John, Thomas and Morgan and also Elizabeth O'Leary Hart, her husband Thomas and their three remaining children Rosalie, Elizabeth and Mary Ann.

The first group of emigrants left home before Christmas in December 1833 on the ship *Prudence.* Power chartered another large sailing vessel the *Heroine* which sailed from Liverpool on 12 March 1834. It was on this ship that Elizabeth Hart and her family sailed. *The Prudence* brought another group of 75 colonists in April 1834.

The route taken was from the Port of Wexford to Liverpool and from Liverpool to New Orleans. James Power and his physically handicapped nephew Martin Power, as well as his sister Elizabeth O'Brien, her husband and family also sailed on the *Heroine.*

The crossing was uneventful until the *Heroine* entered the Bay of Biscay where they encountered a severe storm. The passengers were ordered below deck and the hatches fastened down. On reaching New Orleans the emigrants learned that many of the Colonists awaiting Power's arrival had been stricken with cholera which was then sweeping the United States and Texas.

Rosalie writes:

People were dying so fast that it was impossible to dig graves and the dead were buried in trenches. Two schooners *Sea Lion* and *Wild Cat* were chartered by Power to take the colonists to Aransas Pass.

. . . The schooner *Wildcat* was worthy of her name; she made the trip in forty-eight hours and was wrecked on the end of St. Joseph's Island outside of the bar.

The captain of the *Sea Lion*, on which the Harts were, ran the vessel aground and wrecked her just inside the bar. Luckily no lives were lost but cholera claimed 250 colonists who died and were buried at sea; among them Elizabeth's little daughter Elizabeth.

On landing, the colonists were quarantined on a beach for two weeks to prevent the spread of cholera. Tom Hart, already ill with cholera, died in quarantine and was buried wrapped in a blanket. Elizabeth was now in a strange country, thousands of miles from friends and relations on a sandy beach exposed to the burning heat of the summer sun. All she had left of her family was Rosalie who was not yet eight years old and Mary Ann who was only eighteen months.

After two weeks the colonists were allowed to go to the mission at Refugio, Texas. Everyone had to build primitive houses, with poles for walls and roofs thatched with palmetto or coarse grass. Elizabeth had no one to help with building and was unable to manage. However, she piled up her trunks and farming utensils to form a tent.

Among the dangers to be faced in their new homeland the Harts found snakes in great number including rattlesnakes, copperheads and water moccasins. There were levelling hurricanes and sometimes they endured great cruelty and the killing and scalping of comrades by marauding Indians.

Within six weeks of arrival almost everyone was sick with flux and Elizabeth Hart and another woman cared for the sick and washed their clothes in the river. A man named Robinson hired Elizabeth to help his wife in the house and in return he offered her a field to till. Half the produce of the field was to be returned to him. Elizabeth accepted but the Indians were so hostile that she feared for their lives and returned to the mission.

There, Elizabeth Hart married John James, a widower with three sons. About this time the emigrants became very dissatisfied with the treatment they received from the Mexican Government. The need for social reform caused Texas to rebel against Mexican rule in 1836 and John James joined a company of soldiers to raise the flag of Texan independence in Labardee. He returned once to Elizabeth and took away his sons when he left. There appears to have been no trace of the James family afterwards.

The women and children had to leave the mission for safety and before leaving they buried their valuables. As soon as they left, every house at the Mission was burned. They arrived in total destitution in Victoria.

At Demmit's Landing on the Guadalupe River, Elizabeth found employment as a cook in an eating house which was run by "a negro family". While there, news arrived of the massacre of the Alamo. They tried unsuccessfully to build a raft on which to escape across the river but with the help of two strangers from Kentucky got aboard a skiff just in time to escape the Mexicans and Indians who were in hot pursuit. When they reached the other side, the men seeing that they had neither bedding nor money gave little Mary Ann a five dollar gold piece and threw them a blanket. This was all their earthly possessions.

On their journey to Texas, Elizabeth and her two daughters were on a steamer on the Mississippi when it collided with another. The steamer was holed and began to sink and all the passengers were transferred to the other steamer.

On reaching Mobile, Elizabeth supported herself and her children by taking in sewing. There yellow-fever broke out and the Harts became ill. Elizabeth survived but Mary Ann died leaving her with but one child of her seven; Rosalie.

Elizabeth resolved to return to Texas in the spring. Her husband John James had not returned from the war and was presumed dead. Aboard the schooner she met a Mr Reid and was preparing for marriage to him when he was taken ill and died.

The war of 1846-1848 ended with a peace treaty in which Texas, New Mexico, Arizona and California ceded to the United States. In 1848 Elizabeth decided to open a store in Corpus Christi. She chartered a small boat in Indianola and bought a cargo of goods for the store. Having found a suitable premises she commenced business. As a result of the wars goods were in scarce supply and merchants were selling at four hundred per cent above cost price. Elizabeth decided to undercut and sold off her stock at two hundred per cent above cost. Having sold her first stock and made good profit, she now was in a position to take a larger stock and her business prospered.

About the year 1859 Rosalie married a Mr Priour, and they had seven children; Julian, Elizabeth, Mary Frances, Ambrose, John, Theodore and Isodore. Mr Priour had a sizable homestead in Mobile and her lifestyle included three servants in her home and a nursemaid for her children. Her brother-in-law Reverend Julian Priour was a professor at Springhill College, New Orleans.

At the outbreak of the Confederate wars, Priour sold the ranch at Mobile at a loss and returned to Corpus Christi with his family.

Later they helped to run the very successful business which Rosalie's mother, Elizabeth Hart, had established. In the years that followed they suffered the loss of thousands of dollars in gold and silver coins in a shipwreck. Thousands of dollars worth of goods in transport were destroyed and along with this they were swindled out of four thousand dollars; making a total loss of sixteen thousand dollars in one year. Because of the war and the blockade they were compelled to discontinue the store.

Elizabeth Hart and the Priour family moved out from Corpus Christi to a ranch owned by Elizabeth, on the Aransas river. The Confederates defended Aransas Pass and held off the Federals for some time. Rosalie writes: "You could see women and children running to the country loaded with chickens, wash-tubs, pots, kettles and every imaginable article that they could carry. . . Mr Priour. . . made a kind of cave in the ditch where he put his money and the most valuable articles we had".

When Elizabeth Hart was about 65 years of age, the stress of her life began to take its toll. Rosalie writes:

> During the last year of her life, I walked four miles and a half, taught school all day and in the evening came home and helped to do the housework for a family of nine persons, and for the greater part of the time for eleven. But towards the end of the year my nervous system became so completely exhausted from the constant work and anxiety that when I would arrive at the schoolroom I would be so weak and tremble so much that I would have to sit down and rest before ringing the school bell. When I found that I could no longer walk so far and teach, I had some bedclothes taken to the school house and slept on benches and cooked my meals the best way I could. I kept the youngest of the children with me. We would go to the school every Monday morning and remain there until Friday evening. . .

> It was impossible to procure provisions for money. . . I succeeded in getting a few bushels of corn, but it was so badly eaten by weavils and so musty that it would make one sick to smell it, yet it was better than nothing. This I ground on a hand mill and sifted the best of the meal to make bread for my mother and my children. The hulls I carried to the schoolroom to make bread for myself; this and coffee was the only food I had during the first two weeks that I was teaching school. . .

Elizabeth Hart died on the 20 December 1863 and was buried under a large oak tree by the Aransas river.

Rosalie and her family returned to Corpus Christi in the middle of winter. They had to camp out two nights in freezing conditions. The journey was seventy to eighty miles along the worst kind of roads. At times, with mud up to the hubs of the wagon wheels, they could go only a few feet at a time, then stop to rest the horses.

When they arrived back in Corpus Christi some of her friends begged her to teach their children in return for which they would furnish her with provisions for her family, as the Federals provided for families who supported their cause. She began to teach in the house in which her mother had formerly kept the store.

Note:

1. Elizabeth Hart's daughter Rosalie was a little girl of about eight years old when she left Ireland. Many years later, when she was advanced in years, she dictated her memoirs to a granddaughter. Therefore it is understandable that there may be errors in the account and the dates. The original handwritten manuscript is in the family of Katherine Charlier Whelan, Corpus Christi, Texas. Details in the above account are from a copy belonging to Patricia Hatch Elwonger.

2. It is interesting to note that in the 1980s, descendants of Elizabeth Hart returned to Ballymoney in search of their roots and in 1996, a party of Texans, directly descended from the Ballygarrett colonists of 1833-4, visited Ballygarrett to find their roots and renew kinship. On that occasion a monument, to commemorate the link, was unveiled in the Churchyard of St Mary's Church, Ballygarrett by the US Ambassador to Ireland, Her Excellency Jean Kennedy Smith.

3. The constitution of the United States, on coming into effect in 1789, was largely federal in character. In the following years numerous tensions arose between the states' rights and those of the Washington Government. During the civil war of 1861-1865, the southern states assumed the title Confederate States, implying that their cause was essentially that of state rights against centralized authority while the northern states kept the title of Unionist or Federalist.

Sources:
Rosalie B. Hart Priour - The adventures of a family of emigrants who emigrated to Texas in 1834 - an Autobiography
Oberste William H Texas Irish empressarios and their colonies (1955)

Doctor Annie C Kissane c1990

Annie C Kissane (1898-1995)

Medical Doctor

Despite her sometimes brusque manner Dr. Annie, as she was affectionately known, was well loved and respected in New Ross where her long working life was spent in the service of her patients. She was born at Mulrankin, County Wexford, on 14 July 1898, at a time when Wexford was commemorating the centenary of the 1798 Insurrection. Her father John Kehoe, a National Teacher and her mother Nora, a Junior Assistant School' Mistress in Mulrankin, had three sons and five daughters all of whom were sent to boarding school and University. One became a Vincentian priest, one a Loreto nun, one a professor of physics and chemistry at Carysfort Training College, one died while a student of dentistry, two became teachers and two became doctors; one of whom was Annie.

The road to her chosen career was not an easy one and she met with strong opposition when she decided to give up her studies for an Arts degree in order to study medicine.

While at medical school she was a classmate of Kevin Barry, the eighteen year old revolutionary student who was hanged in 1916 and she was among the group of medical students who formed outside Mountjoy to say the Rosary at the time of his execution. Later, during the Civil War, when it was difficult to obtain medical attention, she was one of the medical students who attended the wounded.

She began work in General Practice in Killanne in July 1924. In 1928 she was appointed medical officer to the New Ross/Ballywilliam dispensary district; becoming one of the first women dispensary doctors in Ireland.

In the Ireland of 1928, there were many who felt that the post of Dispensary Doctor was not a suitable one for a woman. Woman's place at that time was considered to be "in the home".

A local clergyman led a campaign obtaining signatures to a petition to prevent her taking up the appointment. She fought back however and her appointment was ratified by the County Council, whereupon she took up duty.

In 1935, Annie Kehoe married Eamon Kissane from Moyvane, County Kerry, an Irish language teacher employed by the Gaelic League for counties Wexford and Kilkenny. He subsequently became a Fianna Fail TD for North Kerry and Parliamentary Secretary to Taoiseach Eamon DeValera. They had four children, two daughters Brideen and Nora and twin sons John and Jim.

Conditions under which dispensary doctors worked during the 1930s, '40s and '50s were difficult. Annie's district included the mountain area around New Ross where one snowy night on a call to a remote farm house, her car skidded into a snow filled ditch. Unable to attract attention, she spent the night on the mountain side where a search party discovered her next morning, calmly praying her rosary.

On another occasion, she was called at night to a small roadside tarpaulin tent where a sixteen year old traveller girl was giving birth. With only the headlights of her car and on hands and knees she assisted the young mother at the birth of a baby girl.

Among her duties was the carrying out of post-mortems. In the main, these were on bodies taken from the river Barrow at New Ross. This was done in a small building on the Quay known as the Fish house. With a single Garda standing by she worked alone on a body while the Garda put her lighted cigarette between her lips.

Dr Kissane rejected many of the values of society of her day. Attitudes to the mentally handicapped, who at that time were generally kept out of sight, angered her and she became a founder member of the County Wexford Mentally Handicapped Association. She was also a founder member of New Ross Red Cross Society and during the "emergency"* gave lectures and courses in home-nursing. She attended soldiers who were brought to New Ross

Hospital after their vehicle crashed on their way to the Campile Bombing on 26 August 1940.**

On her retirement in 1968 at seventy years of age, being of deep religious conviction, she became a founder member of the New Ross Branch of the Apostolic Work Society, which organised the making of altar cloths and vestments for the priests.

She died on 11 May 1995 at 97 years of age and is interred in St. Stephen's Cemetery, New Ross.

---

* 1939-1945, the years of World War II were known in neutral Ireland as "the emergency".

** On Monday 26 August 1940 during the lunch time break at the Shelbourne Co-operative Store at Campile all the staff, had left the premises, with the exception of three young women, Mary Ellen Kent (30), her sister Cathleen (26) and Kathleen Hurley (27) who were working in the restaurant. A plane, carrying the black markings of the German Luftwaffe passed overhead and dropped three bombs on the Co-op. The first tore through a galvanized roof, then through a wall but failed to explode. The other two exploded wrecking the Co-op and the three women were killed. The plane dropped two more bombs before leaving the area.

Sources:
The Kissane family
Kitty Redmond, Social Welfare Officer, New Ross
The *New Ross Standard* 15/5/95
The Echo 28/8/40

Anita Lett, née Studdy, as a young woman

Anita Lett née Studdy (1870-1940)

Founder of The United Irishwomen's Organisation later named the Irish Countrywomen's Association

Anita Lett was the daughter of Commander Studdy of the Royal Navy. Educated privately, her passionate interest was in horses and hunting and she was attached to the Bree Hunt. She was a skilled gardener and a talented artist.

Her first marriage was to Captain David Longfield Beatty who farmed at Borodale, Enniscorthy. There was one son of the marriage, Henry Longfield Beatty, who as an RAF Officer, died in an air accident in 1938. David Longfield Beatty was many years senior to Anita and died in 1902.

Anita Beatty bought land in Ballynadara near Borodale and built a bungalow there. In 1909 she married Harold Lett, an Enniscorthy businessman and there were two daughters of the marriage; Anita who married Sir John Francis Ainsworth, Archivist and Historian, National Library of Ireland and Eithne who married Patrick Hickey Ballylane, New Ross.

Anita Beatty Lett was a pioneer in the formation of the United Irishwomens' Organisation, forerunner of the still thriving Irish Countrywomens' Association and Founder of the first Branch in Ireland of that Organisation at Bree, County Wexford on 15 June 1910.

A practical farmer, farming her own land, she had, on the advice of a male relative, attended the Annual General Meeting of the Irish Agricultural Organisation in 1909. She became Vice-President of the County Wexford Farmers' Association and was in close touch with the needs of farmers' and labourers' wives.

She called a Meeting at the home of Sir Horace Plunkett in South County Dublin, to which all interested women were invited to discuss the desirability of forming an all Ireland society. A resolution was passed at this meeting to the effect that where societies dealing with

St Aidan's Hall, Bree, where the ICA began in 1910

the objectives of women already existed, they should be made use of as far as possible to avoid conflict or overlapping.

The United Irishwomen owe that title to Susan Mitchell, sub-editor of *The Irish Homestead*. They adopted the motto "Deeds not words". They found that the institutions already existing in the country were sufficient for women's' purposes if it were possible for women to make use of them. They saw that in order to achieve this, women needed the help of men and men's existing organisations so long as they would be allowed to work without stamping out female individuality.

A provisional committee was set up electing Anita Lett as National President with Constance Pim as Honorary Secretary and Elice Pilkington as Organiser.

This Committee was empowered to undertake the organisation of branches. None of these women had any experience of organisations nor any special training but what they lacked in skills they made up for in determination. They set out to find the way and to secure the services of those who possessed the training they lacked.

Anita Lett formed a committee under the presidency of Lady Power, Edermine, on which the farmers' and labourers' wives along with the "county families" were represented. Rules were drawn up and they set to work to brighten the social life of the district by bringing the people together in the Parish Hall. A flower show was held at Bree on 20 August 1910 which provided funds for working expenses and the Branch was soon able to contribute to the expenses of running the Parish Hall.

Women were set to work at skills such as needlework, embroidery, lace, crochet, dressmaking, knitting, spinning and weaving. Classes were organised and women were encouraged to help and educate each other in all the practical skills and to learn the value of work and pride in good work.

Since the Jubilee nurses of that time worked only in the towns, two girls from the Bree area were sent by the organisation to train as nurses in London in order that they could return to work as district nurses in the homes around Bree. These were Margaret Cowman of Sparrowsland, Bree who later became Mrs Breen of Wilton and Annie Foley of Dranagh who married Michael O'Leary of Davidstown.

On 6 December 1910, Mrs Lett formed a second branch of United Irishwomen at Davidstown and by 1911 there were seven branches of the United Irishwomen's Organisation throughout Ireland. Their motto was "Relief from all our troubles will only come from within ourselves. Don't wait to be helped - do it yourself".

The Constitution of the United Irishwomen was as follows:

The Society consists of a central union and branches; the whole governed by an Executive Committee

The work of the central union is first of all to organise the women of Ireland by the formation of branches, as the parent body of the co-operative movement has so largely succeeded in organising the men

Those wishing to join the central union as individual members are proposed and seconded by existing members and are elected by a majority of votes at a meeting of the Executive Committee

Their annual subscription is 2s 6d

Branches are formed in rural districts comprising all the women of the neighbourhood and are governed by a committee composed of a president, vice-president, honorary treasurer, honorary secretary and twelve members

Each branch pays an affiliation fee to the central union of 5s and each member of a branch pays a subscription of 6d to her branch

The Executive Committee is composed of representatives of the branches and individual members who meet in Dublin and deal with all questions that concern the Society

The Executive Committee in 1911 were: Mrs Harold Lett (President), Mrs Alfred Hamilton (Vice-president), Miss Constance Pim (Honorary Secretary), The Countess of Fingall, The Hon Mary Lawless, Mrs Stopford, Mrs Elice Pilkington, Mrs Stephen Spring Rice, Mrs AJ Crichton, Mrs Helen Warren, Miss Helena Kelly,

Miss Beatrice O'Brien, Miss Susan L Mitchell and Miss Purdon. The treasurer was Mr EA Stopford.

About 1928, Anita Lett, assisted by Mabel Rudd, Ballycarney set up a co-operative called Slaney Weavers. Spinning wheels were supplied to women who worked in their own homes. The tweed produced, which was of a high standard, was collected at the Enniscorthy Co-operative Agricultural Society each week. Anita Lett found a sales outlet for the tweed through her sister who lived at Newbury in England.

Anita Lett died in 1940, at the age of seventy and is interred in Clonmore, Bree, Enniscorthy.

The United Irishwomen changed the name of the organisation in April 1935 and became known as the Irish Countrywomen's Association (ICA). There are almost a thousand branches throughout the twenty six counties of Ireland to-day (1998) with 23,000 members.

Sources:
Anita Lady Ainsworth,
Horace Curson Plunkett The United Irish Women and their place, work and ideals (Dublin 1911)
Ann Corrigan, Irish Country Women's Association.
Patrick Hennessy Davidstown Courtnacuddy (A Wexford Parish) (1982)

Elizabeth McGarry at the age of 95

Elizabeth McGarry (1890-1986)
Hotelier

Her approach to business was a personal one. She welcomed each visitor as a special guest and remembered their personal preferences. She believed in serving wholesome home-produced fresh food and would undertake any job, big or small, in the running of her business. Elizabeth was born on 26 December 1890. She was a daughter of Michael Kinsella and Alice Tobin, who farmed at Drummond, Ballyellis. She had three brothers Michael, Tom and Garrett and two sisters Mary and Alice.

She received her education in the local National School and in her younger days worked in Kellett's Fashion and Drapery Stores in Dublin. During these years, she earned five shillings per week and after paying for her lodgings and her train fare home she had only the price of one postage stamp for a letter home.

In 1926 she married John McGarry, whose family had moved in 1924 to live in Courtown, where they ran a public house on Courtown's main street. John McGarry bought two houses in the square in Courtown and opened them as the Bayview Hotel in 1926. In that year, within a short time of opening, he died as a result of an accident.

Elizabeth McGarry, who was expecting her first and only child, John who was born in 1927, continued single-handed to run the hotel. Having cleared all expenses she had one shilling profit after her first year's trading. Over the years she extended and developed the hotel by ploughing back her annual profits.

Along with the management of the hotel, she ran a corner shop selling ice cream and souvenirs. During the emergency years 1939-45 she made all the household soap used in the hotel. This was done by rendering the fat and straining the sediment from the drippings of the roast meat and adding caustic soda dissolved in water. The mixture was put to set in wooden boxes and when set was cut into bars with a fine wire. It made tolerable soap for scrubbing.

In 1951 the hotel was up-graded; the wash stand with jug and basin was discarded and hand basins, with hot and cold running water, were installed in the bedrooms. A new dining room was added on to the hotel and as the business expanded, Elizabeth extended and improved the hotel's facilities; adding a second floor in 1969 with some en-suite bathrooms.

Along with her involvement in local tourist-related affairs she was also a founder and a life-long member of the Riverchapel Branch of the Pioneer Total Abstinence Association and was Hon Secretary of

Advertising running water in the 1950s

the branch for many years. Although committed to total abstinence from alcohol, nothing was allowed to impinge on the practical business management of her hotel. Business demanded a residents' bar and despite her abhorrence of alcohol, this was provided in 1969 also. In the 1980s newly extended kitchens, dining rooms and bar made the Bayview one of the leading hotels in the South East.

Along with rearing her son John, who married Josephine Lawlor, Elizabeth McGarry fostered two of her nieces; Vera Breen, who joined a religious Order and Betty Kinsella, who married Arthur Quinn, Carnew.

She attended Mass daily and was a very active member of the local Praesidium of the Legion of Mary. The family rosary was prayed every night at bed-time in the Bayview Hotel during her lifetime. All year round, irrespective of the weather, she sea-bathed in the early morning.

Fair minded and thrifty, her motto was "I won't do you, but you won't do me either". She held the reins and continued working in the family-run hotel up to the evening before her death, at 95 years of age, on 6 August 1986.

Elizabeth McGarry is interred in Ardamine.

Sources:
The Guardian 13/8/1986
Josie McGarry
Betty Quinn

First Lady Phyllis O'Kelly c1950

Phyllis O'Kelly, née Ryan (1895-1983)

First Lady

Phyllis O'Kelly was the first wife of a President of Ireland to live at Áras an Uachtaráin. Daughter of John Ryan, farmer, Tomcoole, Taghmon and Eliza Sutton, she was the youngest child in a family of four boys and eight girls. Born on 28 February 1895 she was educated in the local National School and in Loreto Abbey, Gorey. Among the first women to attend the National University she was granted a Master of Science degree and worked as an analytical chemist.

She set up her own business as a Public Analyst at Dawson Street Dublin and was employed by the Industrial Research Council, Wexford County Council and many other local authorities. She was also responsible for the analysis of milk for Dublin Corporation.

Phyllis became captain of Ranelagh Craobh Cumann na mBan and served on active duty in the General Post Office during Easter week 1916 when she was twenty-one years old. That week, on Easter Monday 1916 the GPO and other buildings in Dublin were seized by Pearse and Connolly and the Irish Republic was proclaimed. Phyllis Ryan carried despatches for Padraig Pearse from the GPO during the Rising.

In 1936 she married Seán T O'Kelly who previously had been married to her older sister, Mary who died in 1934. From then on, she preferred to be addressed by her name in Irish *Phyllis Bean Ui Cheallaigh*. In 1945, Seán T O'Kelly became Uachtarán na hEireann, succeeding Douglas Hyde. Phyllis gave up her laboratory and went to reside at Áras an Uachtaráin. Work was badly needed on the decaying building and with little money and the co-operation of the architect Raymond McGrath from the Board of Works, she set about making the Áras a place where one could live with a degree of comfort.

Seán T. O'Kelly remained in office until 1959, when the O'Kellys retired to private life in County Wicklow. Throughout the presidency of her husband, Phyllis was described as a "benign and affable first lady".

Phyllis O'Kelly was a member of a family which contributed greatly to Irish life. The contribution of the Ryan family was summed up in a commemorative article on the 75th anniversary of the 1916 Easter Rising:

> The remarkable contribution of a County Wexford farming family to the history, the politics and the scholarship of twentieth century Ireland is well known.

> The Ryan family of Tomcoole were involved in the national movement from the earliest days; their subsequent roles remarkable by any standard in any country in the world. It is likely in the hopeless years of the century's first decade that one of the Ryan girl's destiny would have been impossible to imagine: Phyllis became the wife of Seán T O'Ceallaigh, President of the internationally recognised Republic of Ireland, while Ellen (Nell) Ryan was active in Cumann na mBan in County Wexford and three other sisters were actively involved in Dublin. The most poignant element in their involvement was that Mary Josephine (Min) was the fiancee of the executed 1916 leader Seán MacDermott.

Phyllis O'Kelly died on 19 November 1983 at 88 years of age and is buried in Glasnevin cemetery with her husband Seán T O'Kelly.

Sources:
Betty Glavey and the Ryan family
ET Williams & CS Nicholls eds *The Directory of National Biography 1961-1970*; .
Oxford Univ. Press (1981)
Unnamed paper cutting property B Glavey (28/3/1991)
The People (Wexford) 25/11/1983 p19

Elice Pilkington, (née Esmonde)

Elice Pilkington, Ballinastragh, Gorey, was the sister of Sir Thomas Esmonde, 11th Baronet and Colonel Laurence Esmonde 13th Baronet who succeeded his nephew. She had two other brothers, Walter and John and one sister Annette who married Sutherland Wilkinson, the originator of Titania's Palace.

In 1896, Elice married Colonel Henry Pilkington, Tyrellspass, County Westmeath and there were two daughters of the marriage; Elice Moira who married Theobald Hinkson and Annette who married Richard McGonigal SCM.

She became a founder member and National Organiser of the United Irishwomen and one of its most gifted and energetic personnel. At a time when the Irish Co-operative system was thriving she was aware that there was a necessity for a similar women's movement. The aim was that the rural population of Ireland should be strong, healthy and active.

As a member of the first executive committee, Elice Pilkington undertook the organisation of branches of the United Irishwomen's

Organisation throughout Ireland and set up the second branch to be established in the country; the first having been started in Bree on 15 June 1910. On 3 December 1910 she travelled to Dungloe, County Donegal. Dungloe already had a flourishing co-operative society; a knitting industry in the hands of the women and girls and all round them great possibilities for cottage gardening, dairying and jam making, a village hall for social meetings and a people who were bilingual. Yet there was a depression due to the number of young women and girls emigrating to America.

The proposal to start a branch of the United Irishwomen's organisation was welcomed in Dungloe. A Committee was formed and within one year there was a busy branch there with over 200 members. Two instructresses under the home improvement scheme gave courses and lectures on household economy, home dairying and cottage gardening. The village hall became the centre for meetings of all kinds. The aim was to stem emigration and migration to the towns and to offer the women employment and amusement at home.

Classes of all kinds were offered. Concerts, drama, debates, music, the Gaelic revival and Feis Ceoil were fostered. Country sports, meetings and flower shows were organised along with any gatherings which tended to encourage community friendship and cordial co-operation.

On 7 and 8 December 1910, Elice Pilkington visited Oylegate and Glenbrien in County Wexford to initiate branches. She also visited Bree in order to study the methods of that branch and the pioneer work that had been done by Mrs Lett. The work proposed for the women of rural Ireland came under three headings: agriculture, dairying and cottage gardening.

Agriculture; raising poultry, marketing poultry and eggs, pig rearing: the feeding and care of which already depended largely on women.

Dairying: selling milk, making and selling butter and the correct use of these commodities for home consumption, keeping farm accounts, entering exhibits in agricultural shows in the knowledge that wholesome competition stimulates.

Cottage gardening: bee-keeping; cider-making.

Women were encouraged to support Irish industries by the co-operative purchase of blankets, tweeds, material for clothing, boots and harness. The revival of skills in cottage industries such as basketmaking, rushplaiting, mat and hatmaking, woodcarving, carpentry, designing, cabinetmaking, needlework, embroidery, lace, crochet, dressmaking, knitting, spinning and weaving was encouraged.

Personal neatness and tidiness in the home, thrift, regularity, wholesome and suitable cooking, the use of good materials for cooking, proper diet for children and invalids and good laundry work were encouraged.

Mutual help between women in bringing up their children healthy in body and mind was promoted and co-operation between home and school fostered.

On 10 February 1911 Mrs Pilkington started on a tour through Waterford, Tipperary, Cork and Clare to introduce the ideals of the United Irishwomen's Organisation. She studied the problems of education, domestic economy and public health with a view to having them worked on by the organisation. Seven branches of the United Irishwomen's Organisation existed in 1911.

Elice Pilkington was an accomplished water colourist and for many years was secretary of the Irish Water Colourists Organisation which mounted exhibitions at Mill's Hall, Merrion Row Dublin. She also co-operated with Sir Horace Plunkett in the writing of *The United Irishwomen and their place, work and ideals*.

She is interred in the Pilkington family vault at Tyrellspass, County Westmeath.

Sources:
Alec Hinkson
Horace Curson Plunkett *The United Irishwomen and their place, work and ideals* (Dublin 1911)

The County Hall, Wexford

Ellen (Nell) Ryan (1881-1959)

Republican;
Member Wexford County Council

Ellen Ryan, daughter of John Ryan, farmer, was born in Tomcoole on 5 July 1881. She was fourth eldest in a family of twelve; eight girls and four boys. All eight girls were educated in the local national school and Loreto Abbey Gorey.

Nell spent some years in Germany as a Governess but achieved fame for her part in the struggle for Ireland's Independence and her work in the preparation in County Wexford for the Easter 1916 Rising. During the Rising she was arrested and held in Mountjoy in a cold damp cell without lighting or heating because the Volunteers had cut off the gas supply.

Still incarcerated, on 14 June 1916 she wrote to a friend:

For many reasons I wanted to write to you ever since I came in here. Lately I expected my release every day and was waiting to regain my liberty to send you a line. Now I am beginning to lose hope of a speedy release so am fulfiling a long neglected duty. I always wanted to tell you how sorry I was for you when your dear mother died for I understood all she was to you. I had then laid out to be for certain at The Month's Mind* but my future was taken out of my own keeping. I hope you and all are quite well and really got over your trouble.

Katie and Kathleen Browne were released on Sunday 4 inst. and we have been looking out for our liberty every day since, but each day's sun sets on disappointed hopes. However I was very happy once Katie was set free for she looked so badly. I was afraid she would not be able to stand it much longer. I am very well DG and in the best of spirits. We have had a great lot of experiences since I left Wexford and when I see you again I shall be able to entertain you with a lot of new stories. One of my first visits will be to Foulksmills - for apart from my strong desire for old associations' sake to go there - necessity will bring me. My clothes are quite worn out so I mean to buy some material in Dublin and go straight to Mrs Toomey.

Ellen (Nell) Ryan,
Tomcoole, Taghmon

Chris came up to see us this week and had lots of good news from home. Alice is crossing over to England tonight to visit Jem and all our other friends who are in prison there.

We have no complaints to make of our treatment here but of course one must remember prison at any time is not home.

Most of my old friends have been most kind to me. We got lovely boxes of sweets and all kinds of nice things from all parts.

There are only five of us women prisoners here now. We may get out any day. I told everyone to leave off writing to me. Katie is back at work again. If I get out any of these days I shall remain a little while with her before going home.

With love to Willie and self. Don't forget the poor convict in your prayers. Hoping to see you soon, Yours affectionately, Nelly.

PS Just now Father Owen has been to see me. I was delighted. It was so good of him to look me up. He is very cheerful about Denis. I am so glad there is nothing serious. N.

Mountjoy H. Prison.
14-6-'16.

My dear Lizzie

For many reasons I wanted to write to you ever since I came in here. Lately I expected my release every day and was waiting to regain my liberty to send you a line. Now I am beginning to lose hope of speedy release so am fulfilling a long neglected duty. I always wanted to tell you how sorry I was for you when your dear mother died for I understood all she was to you. I had then laid out to me for certain at the Month's Mind but my future was taken out of my own keeping. I hope you and all are quite well and really got over your trouble.

Katie and Kathleen Browne were released on Sunday 4th inst., as we have been looking out for our liberty every day since, but each day's sun sets on disappointed hopes. However I was very happy once Katie was set free for she looked so badly I was afraid she would not be able to stand it much longer. I am very well D.G. and in best of spirits. She has had a great lot of experiences since I left Mountjoy and when I see you again I shall be able entertain you with a lot of new stories. One of my first visits will be to Jonesmills - for apart from my strong desire for old associations' sake to go there -- necessity will bring me. My clothes are quite worn out so I must to buy some material in Dublin and go straight to our Journey. Chris came up see us this week and had lots of good news from home. She is crossing over to England tonight to visit Jem and all our other friends who are in prison there.

We have no complaints to make of our treatment here but of course one must remember prison at any time is not home. Most of my old friends have been most kind to me. We got lovely boxes of sweets of all kinds of nice things from all parts.

There are only four of us women prisoners here now. We may get out any day. I told everyone to leave off writing some. Katie is back at ... If I get out any of these days I shall remain a little while with her before going home.

With love to Willie and self.

Don't forget the poor convict in your prayers.

Hoping to see you soon.

Your aff...

Nelly

P.S. Just now D. Owen has been to see me. I was delighted. It was so good of him to look me up. He is very cheerful about Denis - I am so glad there is nothing serious. N.

Ellen Ryan's letter from Mountjoy Prison, dated 14/6/16

The prisoners were transferred to Lewis Jail in England on 20 June 1916 and early in August 1916, Nell was transferred to the women's prison in Ailesbury. Countess Markieviez was in Ailesbury Prison at the same time but, as a convicted person, the Countess was held in solitary confinement.

On her release from prison, Nell Ryan immediately resumed her activities in the struggle for Independence. From 1918 to 1922 she was secretary of the Comhairle Dáil Ceanntair of Sinn Féin and worked to secure the transfer of Local Government services from British control to the authority of Dáil Éireann.

She was in charge of Cumann na mBan in the South Wexford Brigade area and at great risk to her personal safety ran the gauntlet on many occasions carrying arms and dispatches and assisting men on the run. In 1922 she was arrested and interned again. During this time she was one of the women internees who underwent 34 days hunger strike in the South Dublin Union.

She was an active member of the Fianna Fáil Organisation from its foundation and served as a member on the National Executive where she represented the South Wexford Constituency. She was a member of Wexford County Council at a time when only 13 women were elected out of a total of 687 seats on 27 County Councils throughout Ireland. She retired from the County Council in 1954 due to failing health.

During her years in public life, she was chairman of the old Wexford Board of Health until it was abolished. She served on the County Wexford Library Committee and the County Wexford Vocational Educational Committee. She was also a member of the County Executive of the Irish Red Cross Society along with being a keen and enthusiastic member of the Hy Cinnsealaigh Historical Society. She was also a member of Wexford Harbour Board.

Always dressed in clothes made of Irish tweeds and linens, Nell Ryan, as she was popularly known, was fearless in debate, outspoken and conscientious, stoutly defending her arguments for the betterment of all classes and creeds. She was straightforward and advocated improved housing and better living conditions for the people. She was said to be highly intelligent, incisive in speech, quick in repartee yet possessing a good sense of humour. For nearly half a century she left the impress of her strong character on the public life of County Wexford. In her personal life she was generous and unselfish. Her health had suffered as a result of hunger strike during her incarceration in Kilmainham and although for a number of years before her death she had stomach cancer she was never heard to complain.

When, at the age of 78 years Nell Ryan died, on 8 December 1959, her funeral was attended by President Eamon deValera and several Government Ministers. She is interred in Glynn cemetery.

Sources:
Betty Glavey and the Ryan family
The People Wexford 12/12/1959

Mother Benedicta Somers

Margaret Somers, Mother Benedicta
(1810-1855)

Loreto sister

Margaret Somers was born in Ballywilliam near New Ross on 20 July 1810. She was a woman in advance of her time in ecumenism. Her charity and concern for all in need, irrespective of their creed, earned for her the highest regard and influenced several conversions to Catholicism. Most notable among her converts were the Ram family of Gorey and their chaplain Reverend Francis Kirk.

Margaret Somers was the younger daughter of Myles and Mrs Somers. She had one sister Catherine and two brothers; one of whom died young and the other boy was named Francis. Myles Somers died when Margaret was only three years old. By the time she was a teenager her mother had also died.

At the age of twenty-five Margaret decided to join a religious Order and on 16 August 1835 became a Postulant with the Institute of the Blessed Virgin Mary, (IVBM) at Rathfarnham. Margaret took the name Benedicta in Religion.

On 19 December 1837, she pronounced her final vows and on that day her sister Catherine, then in her late twenties, decided to enter the same Novitiate. Catherine became Mother General of IBVM, better known in Ireland as Loreto, on the death of its Irish Founder Mother Teresa Ball.

At an early stage in her religious life Sister Benedicta Somers was placed in charge of the temporary house of Loreto at Bullock Harbour, where the nuns resided while Loreto Abbey, Dalkey was being built. She next became Superior to Loreto Convent, North Great George's Street, Dublin where she was replaced by her sister, Mother Scholastica Somers in 1843.

On 21 June 1843, Sister Benedicta arrived in Gorey to occupy Loreto Abbey, accompanied by four Loreto sisters; two of whom were Wexford women; Mary Ham (1819-1907) (Sister Alphonsa)

Loreto Abbey, Gorey (c.1900)

and Teresa Lambert (1791-1854) (Sister Gertrude); both from New Ross. The others were a sister from Cork, Mary Cribbs (Sister Bibiana) and one from Dublin, Mary Clynch (Sister Vincent).

The newly built, Pugin designed church, which had taken three years to build, had been opened and dedicated on 23 June 1842 and one year later the convent and school were completed and ready for occupancy. On Mother Benedicta's arrival, there was an immediate enrolment of 200 pupils but the demand for places was so great that this number could have been more than doubled had accommodation been available.

The 1840s was a decade of Famine and religious intolerance. Mother Benedicta was a deeply spiritual woman and showed a great awareness of the needs of the people in the Gorey district. She attempted to alleviate the grinding poverty of the people by setting up a work room and obtaining needlework to provide employment for the poor women and girls of the town. The convent doors were always open to hungry people in search of food even at times when the Sisters themselves did not have enough to eat.

Her health began to fail in 1846 but Mother Benedicta continued to work and in December 1854, set up the first Christmas Crib in the Diocese of Ferns and crowds thronged from far and near to visit it.

She died on the 28 September 1855 at 45 years of age and is interred in the Convent grounds at Gorey. It was said of this remarkable and holy woman that "the poor were her chief mourners".

For 150 years the work begun by Sister Benedicta was carried on in the Primary and Secondary schools by the Loreto sisters in Gorey. Their aim was to develop all aspects of students' personality; spiritual, intellectual, social, physical, creative and cultural. In 1993, in keeping with Loreto's concern for the educational demands of the times Loreto Secondary School amalgamated with the Christian Brothers and Vocational Education Schools to form the present twelve hundred plus pupil Community School.

After her death, another great Wexford woman, Mother Aloysia Sweetman, became the next Superior of Loreto Abbey Gorey.

She was a member of the Sweetman family of Ballycourcey, Enniscorthy. In 1866, during her time as superior in Gorey, a foundation from Gorey was established at Wexford at the request of Doctor Furlong, Bishop of Ferns. The nuns who went there took up temporary residence in George's Street and on 2 October 1867 the community moved to their present house on Spawell Road.

On 14 October 1872, a foundation was made from Gorey at Enniscorthy under Mother Gonzaga Barry (c1835-1915). Here Edel Quinn (1907-1944) the Legionary of Mary was educated. Mary Barry, herself an Enniscorthy woman, had been a boarder in Loreto Abbey Gorey in 1848, while Mother Benedicta Somers was Superior. She entered the novitiate in Gorey in 1853.

At the age of forty years Mother Gonzaga was requested by Mother Scholastica Somers (Sister of Mother Benedicta) who was then Superior General of IBVM (Loreto), to take a community to Ballarat, Australia to fulfil the needs of Catholic education in that country. For the next forty years Mother Gonzaga pioneered women's education in Australia. She opened the first Catholic teacher-training college for young women and also pioneered the kinder-garten system. She drew up plans for a Catholic hostel for University women but did not live to see this open in 1918.

During her forty years, Loreto foundations and schools were set up in all Australian states except Queensland. Mother Gonzaga Barry died in Australia in 1915 and is interred in the Loreto Convent grounds at Ballarat.

Sources:
Sister Mary Blake, Central Archivist, IVBM (Irish Branch)
The Link vol 11 No 2 Whit 1985
Link with Loreto 1843-1993 (Gorey 1993)

Nellie Walsh (1913-1997)

Nellie Walsh was renowned as a ballad singer with a vast repertoire of traditional songs and ballads. She was born in Wexford in 1913, daughter of John Walsh who ran a grocery and bar at Wygram and Margaret Hayden from Graiguenamanagh, County Kilkenny. She had two brothers Dr Tom, co-founder of Wexford Festival of Opera and the Arts and John "Sandy" Welsh (sic) who was involved in Theatre and television. Her mother died in 1917 when Nellie was four years old and this had a profound effect on her for many years. She received her education from the Sisters of Mercy and Loreto Convent Wexford, where her exceptional singing talent was first noticed.

Before finishing her leaving certificate, Nellie's father became ill with a terminal disease and after his death in 1931, she took over the running of the business which she carried on for almost thirty years.

About 1930 Nellie Walsh became a member of Enniscorthy Operatic Society and took part in many productions of Light Opera. In 1938 it was decided that Wexford should commemorate the 1798 Insurrection and for this Nellie began her collection of songs and ballads. This was the beginning of her career as a ballad singer. In the 1940s she was invited to sing on Repertory programmes throughout Ireland and had a distinguished career, recording and broadcasting with Radio Éireann and the BBC. She was also well known to Irish emigrants in England; performing before packed audiences throughout Lancashire and elsewhere. She was a member of the Rowe Street Church Choir and was a long-standing member of the Guinness Choir.

Nellie was a leading member of Wexford Festival opera chorus for forty years. She had the honour to be the first soloist to sing in the first Wexford Festival opera *The Rose of Castille* in 1951. Nellie also served on the Festival Council.

Nellie Walsh

In 1973, at sixty years of age she qualified for an LLCM diploma in singing from the London college of Music.

She was a founder member of Wexford Historical Society in 1944 and served on the Society's committee in various capacities. In 1989 she was elected President and her outstanding personal contribution was acknowledged in 1990, when made an Honorary Life Member.

She wrote her *Memoirs of Wexford*, part of which were published, in 1992, in *Wexford Through its Writers*. For many years she was a columnist in the *Free Press* and later *Ireland's Own*. In 1996, she published her autobiography *Tuppences were for Sundays*.

She died at Ely House Hospital, Wexford on 8 June 1997 and is interred in Barntown cemetery.

Sources:
The Echo 11/6/1997,
Nicky Furlong - *The Echo* 26/6/1997
Nellie Walsh *Tuppences were for Sundays* (1996)

Jane Francesca Lady Wilde (c1822-1896)

"Speranza" of The Nation

She was born in Wexford in the early 1820s. Evidence of the date of her birth is difficult to obtain. It is thought to be c 1822 as her father Charles Elgee left Dublin for the East Indies in 1822 and his death there was reported in the *Freeman's Journal* 4 February, 1825. Her genealogy is set out by RJ Elgee, a kinsman, as follows:

> The Very Reverend John Elgee was the son of Charles Elgee, whose wife's name was Alice Corran. John Elgee, married Jane Waddy of Clougheast in 1785, being then 32 years of age.

> In 1793 John Elgee was appointed Curate of the Parish of St Selskar, Wexford and in 1796 was appointed Rector of that Parish and so remained until his death in 1823. (It would appear that at this time the Parish was known as the Parish of St Selskar and not the Parish of Wexford).

There were six children of the above marriage and I think it is only necessary to deal with three of them:

(1) Jane Elgee born 1787 married on the 20th February 1806, in Castlebridge Church one Robert McClure and there was issue of that marriage one son, Robert John Le Mesurier (McClure) who was born on 30 January 1807, his father predeceasing his birth by some weeks. Robert JL McClure subsequently joined the Royal Navy and was accredited with the discovery of the North West passage. He died, intestate, without issue on 17 October 1873; he was then Rear Admiral Sir Robert McClure KCB.

(2) Richard Waddy Elgee born 7 October 1788, who also entered the Church and was appointed Rector of Wexford Parish in 1845 and so remained until his death in February 1865. (The stained glass East window in St Iberius Church was erected in his memory). Richard Waddy Elgee married in 1820 Cassandra Hawkshaw of Clones and had eight children one of whom, Richard Waddy Elgee, born in 1837, became a solicitor in 1861 and in that year joined with Simon Little to form the firm of Little & Elgee. He married Susan Boxwell daughter of Dr Boxwell of Infirmary House, in 1864 and had, inter alia, my father John Elgee, who was born in 1875. My father married Magdalene Toole of Curracloe House in 1911 and he died in 1953.

(3) Charles Elgee was born 1791 and married in or about 1820 Ann S Kingsbury and of this marriage there were two daughters Emily Thomazine who married a man named Warren and Jane Francesca Anne who was born in Dublin in or about the year 1823 (the exact place or date of birth has not been traced) Jane Francesca Anne married William Wilde and they had three children, one of whom was Oscar Wilde, as he is most commonly called.

In the biography entitled *Speranza* by Horace Wyndham published in 1951 it was stated that: "Charles (Elgee), a Wexford Attorney, who married a Miss Kingsbury, was her father. She had no sisters, and her only brother, anxious to improve his position went to America. There he took out papers of naturalization, and joining the New York Bar, eventually became a Judge". RJ Elgee disputes this and claims:

With regard to the extract from Horace Wyndham's biography, I have nothing to show what Charles Elgee was and so can neither confirm or deny that he was an attorney as described.

With regard to the question as to whether Lady Wilde had a brother or sister, my information as conveyed to you is correct that she had one sister only; apart from other documents and letters I have been assisted by the fact that Sir Robert McClure died intestate, leaving a widow but no issue, with the result that his personal estate was divided between his various relatives with a right of dower to his widow. This matter was dealt with in the Probate Office in London and I have a copy of the Schedule issued showing the persons who were entitled, this includes Lady Wilde and Mrs Warren, as being entitled to the share of their late father. The matter was enlivened by the fact that Sir Robert had been awarded £10,000 (£500, 000 in current values), for his discovery of the North West Passage and the shares were, therefore, quite considerable.

Because her birth was not registered Lady Wilde had difficulty in establishing her credentials in order to claim her inheritance and on 19 October 1894 she wrote to her cousin who was the executor of the will:

There is no register of my birth in existence. It was not the fashion then nor compulsory in Ireland as it is now. But I cannot see why it is required when there is no dispute as to my identity as daughter of Charles Elgee. I know that when my mother came in for money by the death of Sir Thomas Ormsby, intestate, the certificate of her birth was not required. If the register of my parents marriage would suffice, it is in the Wexford Parish Book and with this the Register of my marriage as Jane F Elgee can also be handed in proving I was truly this person.

The general consent of all the family is always considered enough to establish the right to a name and relationship.

The family can also give an oath that I am the youngest daughter of Charles Elgee, eldest son of Archdeacon Elgee and Ann Sarah Kingsbury, his wife, married in Wexford by your father.

Yours as ever

Jane Francesca Wilde

The Elgees were a Protestant Unionist family of builders, clergymen and attorneys. Jane was taught by a succession of governesses and tutors and had a sound knowledge of French, German and Italian along with the ability to read Latin and Greek "for pleasure" at an early age.

Her main interests were politics and history and influenced through the promotion of a new type of nationalism by the Young Irelanders, Jane Elgee began contributing to the *Nation*. This newspaper founded by Young Irelanders Thomas Davis, John Dillon and Charles Gavin Duffy sought to promote unity among Protestant, Catholic and Dissenter. Initially she wrote under a male pseudonym "John Fenshaw Ellis" but it was as "Speranza" that her fame has endured and she published a volume of poems under that nom de plume.

In the 1840s, her essays and verse writings were intensely nationalistic and inflammatory and many such as the following were written in the "heroic mode".

> Oh that I stood upon some lofty tower
> Before the gathered people face to face
> That like God's thunder might my words of power
> Roll down the cry of freedom to its base!
> Oh, that my voice, a storm above all storms
> Could cleave earth, air and ocean, rend the sky
> With fierce shout "To Arms To Arms"
> For Truth, Fame, Freedom, Vengeance, Victory.

She deplored the state of poverty and deprivation among the masses of the people on the eve of the Great Famine. In 1848, she wrote a leading article in *The Nation*. It was in fact a prose poem entitled *Jacta Alea Est* (The die is cast). It has been described as "a wild war song in which Ireland was called upon that day in the face of earth and heaven to invoke the *ultima ratio* of oppressed nations".

That issue of *The Nation* in which it appeared on 29 July 1848 was suppressed by the Castle authorities and in 1849 when Charles Gavan Duffy was prosecuted for seditious writing and in particular *Jacta Alea Est*, Jane Elgee sitting unsuspected in the public gallery stood up and announced "I am the criminal, who as author of the article that has just been read should be in the dock. Any blame in respect of it belongs to me". The statement was accepted and the charges against Duffy were dropped.

In 1851 she married Sir William Robert Wills Wilde, a distinguished Dublin surgeon and antiquarian who was knighted by

1894 letter from Jane Francesca Wilde to her cousin

Queen Victoria. They took up residence at 21 Westland Row and there William was born in 1852 followed by a second son Oscar, in 1854. Four years later a baby daughter, Isola Francesca was born.

The Wildes moved to a larger house at 1 Merrion Square North where Lady Wilde emulated the French salon, inviting to her home all the distinguished members of Dublin's educational and cultural society and also all those who had the slightest affiliation with literature and the arts. She dressed in a spectacular manner; sometimes in flowing classic robes and at other times in rustling silk and lace flounces with wreaths of golden leaves adorning her hair. Brooches and bracelets ornamented the ensemble and when greeting her guests she wore white kid gloves and carried a dainty handkerchief and scent bottle.

Jane Wilde was intensely fond of her children and children's parties were often held in Merrion Square. Her daughter Isola died in the Spring of 1867 at ten years of age.

After the death of her husband in 1876, Lady Wilde moved to London where she began writing for the *Pall Mall Gazette* under her own name. Sir William Wilde left £8,000 to his wife and £4,000 each to his sons Willie and Oscar. He also left £4,000 to Henry Wilson, his first natural child.

Despite the success of her son Oscar and her own publications the last years of Lady Wilde's life were dogged by ill-health, poverty and increasing loneliness. In 1890 a Civil List Pension of £70 per annum was awarded to Lady Wilde. This was a welcome supplement to her meagre income.

In her twilight years Oscar's son, Vyvyan Holland described her as:

a terrifying and very severe old lady, seated bolt upright in semi-darkness, while the sun shone brilliantly outside. She was dressed like a tragedy queen, her bosom covered with brooches and cameos. The curtains all through the house remained permanently drawn and the drawingroom was lit by guttering candles, arranged in the corners of the room, as far away from my grandmother as possible so that the heavy make-up with which she tried to conceal her age could not be detected.

I protested strongly every time I was taken to pay her a duty visit; even when many years later, I lived in Oakley Street myself I never passed that part of the street without a sense of foreboding.

This was in stark contrast to AM Sullivan who, in his book *The New Ireland*, written in 1877, described her as "young, beautiful, highly educated, endowed with the rarest gifts of intellect, her personal attractions, her cultivated mind, her originality and force of character, made her the central figure in Dublin society thirty years ago".

In the Spring of 1896 she caught a chill and already run down in health, complications set in. On 3 February 1896 her landlady, on entering her bedroom, found her dead. Her last resting place is an unmarked grave in Kensal Green Cemetery in the Paddington district of London.

At the time of her death *The Nation* was being published as *The Irish Catholic and Nation*. On 15 February 1896 *The Irish Catholic and Nation recorded*:

It is with feelings of deep regret that we have to chronicle the death which occurred last week of Lady Wilde ("Speranza" of the Nation) whose fervent love of Ireland - a love that lasted onto death - found manifestation in impassioned verse and on at least one memorable occasion in most eloquent prose. That hers was a deeply religious as well as patriotic nature is attested by many passages in her poetry. That in death she has found those aspirations, which Protestant though she was, have been fulfilled, will be the prayer of all the children of the Old Land which she loved so dearly.

A friend of "Speranza", P Magennis wrote a lengthy poem entitled "Lines on the death of Lady Wilde" which was published in *The Northern Patriot* in 1896 and is telling of her character and friendship:

No cloud she raised to dim another's light
No narrow thoughts, no jealousy inspired
To censure others or have herself admired
But spreading light and dissipating gloom
She, genius, where she found it, bade it bloom.

Books by Speranza - Lady Wilde:

Sidonia the Sorceress (1849)
Pictures of the First French Revolution (1850)
The Wanderer and his home (1850)
The Glacier Land (1852)
The First Temptation (1853)
Poems by Speranza (1864)
Poems: Second Series; Translations (1866)
Memoir of Gabriel Beranger (Continuation) (1880)
Driftwood from Scandinavia, a travel book (1884)
Ancient Legends, Mystic Charms and Superstitions of Ireland (1887)
Ancient Cures, Charms and Usages of Ireland (1891)
Notes on Men, Women and Books (1891)
Social Studies (1893).

Sources:
Irene Elgee
Horace Wyndham: *Speranza - A Biography of Lady Wilde* (London 1951)
Irish Catholic and Nation 15/2/1896
Letters of RJ Elgee, Little & Elgee, Solicitors, Wexford to Edward O'Brien published in the *Journal of the Wexford Historical Society* vol vii 1978-9 pp50-70
Northern Patriot - Shan Van Vocht, MF Reel 1 1896-1899 National Library of Ireland

Note:
The Irish Catholic and Nation re-issued under the title *The Nation* in 1896 and the first number under the old title appeared on Saturday 6 June 1896.

Sources

Primary Sources

Personal interviews

Manuscript collections:

Nicholas Cosgrave
Irene Elgee
Betty Glavey
Patricia Hatch Elwonger

Newspapers:

The Echo 1940, 1997. 1998
The Guardian 1980, 1996
The Irish Catholic and Nation 1896
The Irish Times 1997
The New Ross Standard 1995
The People (Wexford) 1898, 1959, 1964, 1978, 1983
The Shan Van Vocht 1896-9 vol i No 3 M/F NLI

Periodicals:

Kilmore Parish Journal No 24 1995-6
The Link - Gorey Newsletter vol 11 No 2 Whit 1985, vol 15 No 2 Whit 1989
Link with Loreto 1843-1993 (Gorey 1993)
Mashonaland Irish Association Centenary Year Booklet (1991)
Old Wexford Historical Society Journal 1978-9 vol vii
The Pioneer June 1991
RIAI Yearbook 1975
150th Anniversary Publication of RIAI (1989)

Printed Sources:

Doris Burton, *Heroic Nuns* (1965)

Bernard Browne, *County Wexford connections* (Published Wexford)

Byrne Des, 'Mother Patrick -The first Irishwoman in Zimbabwe' in *The Pioneer* (June 1991)

MT Connolly, *Forty Years of Wexford Agriculture* (1996)

Comerford Máire, *The First Dail* (Dublin 1969)

Anna Day, *More than one egg in the basket (History of the Munster Institute* (1992)

AJ Dachs and WF Rea, *The Catholic Church and Zimbabwe 1879–1979* (1980)

Charles Dickson, *The Wexford Rising in 1798* (Tralee 1956)

Dominican Sister, *In God's white-robed army* (1947)

Michael Fitzpatrick, *Historic Gorey* iv vols, 1987, 89, 95, 98

Michael Gelfand, *Mother Patrick and her nursing sisters* (1964)

PF Kavanagh, *A popular history of the Insurrection of 1798* (1898)

Margaret MacCurtain and Donnacha O'Corrain eds. *Women in Irish Society (The historical dimension)* (1978)

Mary McNeill *The life and times of Mary Ann McCracken (1770-1866)* (1988)

SW Myers and D McKnight eds *Richard Musgrave Memoirs of the Irish Rebellion of 1798* (Indiana 1995)

William H Oberste, *Texas Irish empressarios and their colonies* (1955)

Horace Curson Plunket, *The United Irishwomen and their place, work and ideals* (Dublin 1911)

AM Sullivan, *The new Ireland* (1877)

George Taylor, *Rebellion in Wexford in the year 1798* (Dublin 1800)

Nellie Walsh, *Tuppences were for Sundays* (1996)

ET Williams and CS Nicholls eds: *The Directory of National Biography 1961-70*, Oxford University Press (1996)

Horace Wyndham, *Speranza - A biography of Lady Wilde* (London 1957)

Index